WHEN'S DADDY COMING HOME?

Published in the United States by
Hybrid Global Publishing
301 E 57th Street
4th Floor
New York, NY 10022

Copyright © 2021 by John Cookson

United States rights reserved. No part of this book may be reproduced or transmitted in any form or by any means, electronic or mechanical, including photocopying, recording, or by any information storage and retrieval system, without the written permission of the Publisher, except where permitted by law.

Manufactured in the United States of America.

Margetts, Peter and Cookson, John
When's Daddy Coming Home?
    ISBN: 978-1-951943-75-2
    eBook: 978-1-951943-76-9

Cover design by: Joe Potter
Interior design by: Suba Murugan
Copyediting by: Felice Gill (XCU Agency)

Published by The Conrad Press in the United Kingdom 2020

ISBN 978-1-911546-97-9
Copyright © Peter Margetts and John Cookson, 2020

Typesetting and Cover Design by: Charlotte Mouncey, www.bookstyle.co.uk

WHEN'S DADDY COMING HOME?

A father's quest for freedom from an unjust Dubai life sentence

BY PETER MARGETTS, WITH JOHN COOKSON

For Olivia

CONTENTS

Foreword:

1 - Did you sign this check?	11
2 - The Mad Hatter's Tea Party	32
3 - When did it all go wrong?	41
4 - The early days	63
5 - Life sentence	84
6 - Escape plans	97
7 - Sex, drugs...no rock' n roll	114
8 - Shot at dawn	122
9 - Double sadness	129
10 - Hunger strike	133
11 - Gracias, amigo	164
12 - Death in the afternoon	173

13 - Sheikh Mo	181
14 - Friends in high places	195
15 - Sex on the beach	210
16 - The Pink Panthers	219
17 - Blood money	224
18 - Me versus the Emirates pilots	226
19 - False start	231
20 - Halfway house	238
21 - Glass of champagne, sir?	240
22 - Thanks, Lady A	245
23 - My darling Olivia	247
Postscript	
Final Thoughts by Peter Margetts	251

FOREWORD

In 2008 the crippling world economic crisis hit Dubai.

Billions were wiped off the Emirate's; stock exchange. State-owned industries crumbled in financial ruin. Property prices crashed and construction companies went into liquidation.

Little spoken of victims of Dubai's spectacular economic meltdown included thousands of businessmen and women who'd written post-dated security check which to that were suddenly worthless.

One of them was British-born property developer Peter Margetts who was arrested under Dubai's draconian check laws and thrown into a notorious jail, along with hundreds of other Western expatriates.

For Peter, the night of his arrest was just the start of an unimaginable prison ordeal which to that cost him his marriage and almost his life.

What follows is an incredible but painful, true-life story.

Some names have been changed for legal reasons.

Peter Margetts and John Cookson

1

Did you sign this check?

I will never forget that rotten day.

Monday lunchtime, late January 2009; I'd just wrapped up a meeting with my attorney, Ludmilla, at Dubai's luxury Shangri-La Hotel, when my cellphone rang.

'Peter, you'd better get your arse back to the office, something very urgent's come-up.'

It was my straight-talking business partner, Kieran Beeson. 'What's the problem?'

I sensed someone was breathing down Kieran's neck.

'Look, Peter, please get yourself back, now,' pleaded Kieran, a 'street-wise,' twenty-something.

Minutes later I was in my white Range Rover, foot down, barreling along the Sheikh Zayed Highway to my office in Al Barsha where two men in white *dishdashas* were waiting.

The smiley, older one raised a hand: 'Come on in, Mr. Peter, yes, do come in,' he beckoned.

They were cops from Dubai's Department of Criminal Investigation, an elite force reporting directly to the Ruler of Dubai, Sheikh Mohammed. They investigated everything, from serious white-collar crime, to terrorism and Dubai's underworld.

The two officers weren't the only members of the reception committee.

I hadn't noticed him at first, but one of my clients, a Dane in his mid-thirties, sat grim-faced and arms-crossed, in a corner. He glared at me, but said nothing. He didn't need to.

I'd a fair idea why police had dropped in for a little chat.

I was the boss of a Dubai-based property development company and the Dane was a member of a syndicate of forty-two Emirates airline pilots who'd invested U.S.$7 million in my firm. The money was a loan, to build a luxury apartment complex.

But the entire Dubai economy had recently collapsed. As a result, the apartment construction project went to hell in a handcart and the pilots lost their life savings. I didn't escape the carnage. My firm had gone bust and I was effectively bankrupt.

The meeting earlier with my lawyer had been about cobbling together a financial rescue package for the Emirates flyers.

'OK, chaps, how can I help?' I inquired with a smile.

'Mr. Peter, we're taking you for questioning to Bur Dubai police station,' said the older officer.

Now, as any old Dubai hand knew, in a potentially dodgy situation with Emirati cops, it paid to remain smiling and polite and normally any problem; or *mushkela,* in Arabic; was smoothed over, especially for a Western expat.

As far as I knew I'd committed no crime, so I assumed we'd trot along to Bur Dubai, have a chin-wag over a glass of sweet tea, clear up any *mushkela* and I'd be back home in time for dinner with my lovely wife, Susan, and a cuddle with our two-year-old daughter, Olivia, our little princess.

I followed the police in my own car, as they'd asked me to, for the fifteen-mile drive to Bur Dubai, where I was ushered into an interrogation room and invited to sit down.

One of the CID officers immediately dived into a file and waved a post-dated security check in front of my nose. It was one of forty-two check I'd signed and handed to the pilots, as per my agreement with them.

'Did you sign this check, Mr. Peter? It's bounced. There's no money in your account.'

I am a straight-batting sort of guy and there was no point denying it: 'Yes, of course that's my signature, definitely. My company collapsed, that's why there's no money, the pilots know that,' I replied.

Looking back, I wished I'd taken a moment at that point to call to my attorney, Ludmilla, because events took a life-altering twist.

Immediately I nodded I'd signed the bounced check, the two cops ended the interview, told me I'd been arrested, and then escorted me to another interrogation room deeper inside the Bur Dubai police complex, where they locked me in.

The clunking sound of the lock made me feel a as in a chill. Everyone in Dubai was aware of Bur Dubai's sinister reputation for violence among prisoners and for police brutality.

A few years before fourteen prisoners were killed when another inmate set fire to a cell.

Two years after my arrest, Lee Brown, a forty-nine-year-old Brit from London, died in the same police station. The poor devil was found half-naked in his cell; his family claimed he'd been beaten to death during interrogation; the police denied it, and the cause of Lee's demise was never proved.

But, back to events that evening, and I sat on my own, twiddling my thumbs for an hour in the locked interrogation room, then another hour, still wondering what the hell was going on.

Three hours slid by when suddenly there was a noisy commotion; a turning of the locks. Police shoved a crazed-looking young Arab man into the room. Then they secured the doors again.

'Great,' I muttered to myself, 'now you're in a locked Bur Dubai interrogation room with a nut-job.'

The disturbed lad's eyes bulged, his hair was disheveled, his forehead and t-shirt were streaked with dried blood; he'd clearly been in a punch-up and, from his demeanor, I guessed he'd not been taking his meds.

As he paced the floor and ranted, I tried to make conversation as best I could. I established he was Palestinian, and he'd been in a fistfight with another guy for reasons he had difficulty explaining, and I couldn't work out.

I began to worry he might attack me when, suddenly, the doors rattled open again. Another man was bundled in; an Egyptian named Farid who spoke with an American accent.

Farid was an intelligent business person like me, also in his forties, a family man with a kind, handsome face. He explained he'd lived most of his life in the States, but, had recently established himself as a property developer in Dubai, just as I had done before the economy crashed.

'Why have you been arrested? Dud checks?' I asked.

'Yes, my friend,' Farid said, with a half-smile.

I warmed to Farid immediately, his presence made me feel safer. Meanwhile the Palestinian fretted and muttered away in the corner.

We were left alone for another hour until police officers marched in and handcuffed the three of us. I noticed, from my watch, it was nine p.m.

They handed us over to armed police who bustled us out of the building into the metal cage of a security van parked outside.

'Now they now take us to Al Rashidiya police station,' said the troubled Palestinian, who'd been arrested a few times before and knew the drill.

As the van's engine revved and moved off and we bounced around in the cage at the back, I muttered to myself: 'Peter, you're in deep, serious shit now.'

He may have been as mad as a box of frogs, but the Palestinian pugilist was correct about our destination.

We pitched up at Al Rashidiya's massive police detention center where cops ripped the van doors open and screamed at us: '*Yellah! Yellah!*' 'Go! go!'

The three of us scrambled out into Dubai's version of Bedlam. There were hundreds of men in handcuffs and, I realised, we were part of the daily round-up of suspects from police stations across the city. Amid the roar of reversing prison vans, clouds of exhaust fumes, blazing headlights and shrieks from impatient guards, was a heaving mass of prisoners, mostly culled from Dubai's Asian workforce: Indians, Nepalis, Pakistanis, Bangladeshis, Malaysians and Filipinos.

Sticky heat, arc lights, the confused cacophony and sheer numbers of men, young and old; my heart raced; my eyes darted left and right trying to spot another white face, one of my own.

But, I saw no one. On that dark night it seemed I was the only Westerner being herded into the Al Rashidiya Detention Center.

I like to think of myself as strong-willed and at that point I gave myself a pep talk.

'Peter, don't worry. They won't keep you here. The office will call a lawyer and get you bail. This was all a mistake, they'll let you go,' I said under my breath.

Suddenly, a shove in the back and guards pushed me, Farid, and the Palestinian, toward a slow-moving line of prisoners. Some younger ones were sobbing, overwhelmed by what was happening.

Guards yelled at us to hand over valuables and personal items such as cellphones, credit cards, watches, bracelets.

Eventually, I reached the front of the queue still dressed in my business slacks and shirt from earlier that day. I had the equivalent of about U.S.$200 dollars in UAE *dirhams* rolled in my pocket.

The check-in clerk, if I can describe him thus, was, according to his name tag, called Tariq, a chubby Emirati who clearly had an appetite for pies.

He said nothing and leant back in his leather swivel chair to look me up and down with a sneer, like I was the last turkey in the shop. I weighed him up too.

I put him in his early thirties, his military cap was set at a rakish angle, his brown uniform was grease-stained, his massive belly threatened to burst through the straining buttons on his tight tunic.

I sensed he was savoring the moment of having a Westerner in front of him and, without troubling to lean forward and out of his reclining position, he exclaimed: 'Ah-ah! a British man. You're welcome here!'

After fumbling through paperwork his fat fingers reached down to scratch his crotch, then, with eyes glinting, he said: 'Let me tell you something very important, Mr. Peter.

'People in this place, Al Rashidiya, will make you lots of promises, tell you lots of things, but I'm the only one who can give you anything you want; please remember that.'

I almost responded: 'Well, Tariq, that's very nice of you, but I wasn't planning to stay.'

'I can get you anything, anything at all, except one thing.'

He then paused theatrically.

Breaking an awkward silence;

'And what's that?' I asked.

Looking at me with a steady stare and grinning, he replied: 'I can't let you leave this place, OK?'

The previous few hours had been utterly surreal. I was tired, mentally near breaking point, and the guard Tariq telling me I wasn't going home that night, or maybe not at all, had left me devastated.

I was desperate to speak to my beautiful wife, Susan, or indeed any normal person outside the hellhole I'd just been dumped in, but they'd taken my cellphone away.

'Christ, how the hell am I going to get out of this mess?' I said under my breath, as Tariq's plump hand casually flicked me on to the final stage of the check-in process.

By then I'd caught up with Farid and the wild-eyed Palestinian who looked as if he was about to deck some poor bastard, and three of us were taken by elevator to a first-floor landing of the main detention block where guards heaved on a huge, steel door.

It opened to reveal a vision of hell; a vast chamber about seventy-feet long, crammed wall-to-wall with prisoners, many hundreds of them, sprawled across grubby mattresses. A place where all hope was gone.

The smell hit me and I gagged on the acrid stench of stale sweat, urine and human shit. The chamber's walls were stained dark yellow from decades of nicotine.

As my eyes adjusted to the Stygian gloom, I slowly focused on a sea of swarthy faces glaring at back at me; the new boy.

'In you go, Mr. Peter,' said a guard nudging me across the threshold with his elbow. Then, the great door groaned and slammed shut with a metallic thud. There was no escape.

It felt like I'd been thrown into a kind of underworld, and I wandered hesitantly down endless lines of mattresses and men to get my bearings more than anything else.

The first thing I noticed was so many prisoners had an odd, glassy-eyed look, as if they were staring at some unseen distant parallel universe. They were there, but not there. I could have been King Kong wandering amongst them. I doubt it would have registered.

I heard a man cry in pain from a far-off, dark corner, deeper inside.

I pushed on like a jungle explorer, getting the 'lay of the land', and counted ten cells to the right of me with five bunk beds in each. Surely that wasn't enough for the masses of prisoners?

Further in, small bands of Asians, mostly Pakistani youths, their pupils dilated like dinner plates and arms swirling like Dervishes, staggered toward me, babbling away in Urdu. They were obviously off their heads on crack, or some other mind bender. They pushed their wild-eyed faces into mine to take a better look at me.

The fact they'd lost their minds was a blessing in a way because it was easy enough to shove them away. One was so thin, it was like pushing at a sack of dried leaves, so fragile, I felt I could have walked through him.

'Hold it together, Peter, hold it together,' I repeated to myself. 'Keep a grip.'

I pressed on, and at the end of a corridor I came across three filthy lavatories and a couple of makeshift showers. The shitters were simple holes in the ground with a tiled slab over them. No toilet paper, just grubby jugs of water; a scene of indescribable filth really. The smell was so vile I wanted to retch.

Close by, I noticed a small courtyard open to the skies, also packed with inmates, mostly Asian and Arab men, sprawled across more grubby mattresses. Those without a bed were stretched half-asleep on tables in what could have been an eating area.

My recce completed, I estimated there were around 400 prisoners. I guessed some had been arrested for murder, robbery, drug dealing and sex offences like rape. Others were there for what is euphemistically called 'white-collar' stuff, like fraud and embezzlement. I wondered if any were bounced check cases like me?

Having got the geography of the place in my head I retraced my steps. I noticed there was no clock; so no sense of time. There was nothing to read, no distractions, so most of the day and night, I assumed, was spent fending off attackers, sleeping as best you could, eating and praying to God that someone was going to get you out.

For a minute or so, for reassurance, I kidded myself I'd wandered onto a film set and all around me were actors, because that's what they looked like. This could not be real.

But where were the cameras, the director and producer?

No, it wasn't a remake of *Midnight Express*, or even a bad dream.

This horror story was very real, and I was one of the central characters.

I swiveled through a one eighty degree turn and began to wander back toward the main door.

Hundreds of dark eyes had fixed on me, and definitely not in a friendly way

I knew I needed my own bit of personal turf in the chamber of horrors, and, as I scanned around looking for a spare mattress, one inmate caught my eye.

He looked like he was Iranian, he was in his forties, with salt and pepper hair and goatee beard. He was incongruously suited-up, 1970s-style, with an olive-green jacket and matching flared trousers, a mustard shirt, flowered tie, and you couldn't miss his pink, plastic sandals.

Sitting crossed legged on his mattress, like Buddha, he had what the military call command presence, but what, actually, had drawn me to him was his whistling, electric kettle, just coming to the boil.

'Tea?' he asked casually, as if I'd just popped in for a cup of Earl Grey.

'Please sit down here with me, my friend. Make yourself comfortable.'

He shuffled along his mattress to make room and pushed a grubby polystyrene cup toward me.

'So, my friend, you're British, are you? Very good. I like British.'

He handed me a used tea bag and poured boiling water into my cup.

'Well, I must tell you, please be very careful in here my British friend.'

I nearly replied: 'No shit, Sherlock!'

Our conversation flowed, very easily, and I discovered his name was Haj; he was indeed Iranian. Given his attire he surprised me a little by claiming he'd been a highly respected lawyer in Dubai who'd been recently arrested, not because he'd done anything illegal, but because his boss was a fraudster.

I didn't quite get that and didn't inquire further, but I was already enjoying Haj's openness and his warmth, as well as his tea.

He was keen to know how I'd ended up in Al Rashidiya, so I explained the story of my business deal with the syndicate of Emirates pilots which to that had fallen through, how my company had gone bust, how I was bankrupt and the pilots had lost U.S.$7 million of investment.

'Emirates Airlines is part of the government. Best you pay the company's pilots their money back, or you'll be in jail for a very, very long time, my friend. They'll keep you forever if you don't.'

I insisted to Haj I'd done nothing illegal. I told him that my company had got into a mess because of Dubai's economic crash, and I did, indeed, have plans to repay the pilots, as soon as I was freed. First, I needed get out of this place.

'OK my fine Englishman, you do your best with that and good luck.'

We chatted for a few more minutes and then he declared: 'The first priority is to find you a mattress, as you'll be here a while. They're not free. You have to buy one.'

As in the world of real estate I'd left behind, 'location, location, location,' even in Al Rashidiya's hall of horrors, was everything. Mattress placement also settled your status in the inmate pecking order. Those who could afford it were at the posh end, next to the main door, and the destitute were near the bogs.

So, according to Haj, a mattress near the stinking lavatories cost only a handful of *dirhams*, the equivalent of five bucks. But a mattress in prime real estate, close to the big metal entrance door, was the most expensive; up to two hundred bucks each.

Continuing the sales patter: 'By the way, Mr. Peter, you can hot-mattress if you want; share with another prisoner perhaps? Maybe that's for you: twelve hours on, twelve hours off?'

Noting my frown: 'Well, perhaps not then!' he said.

'No thanks, Haj, I definitely need my own mattress.'

'OK, I can find you one, in a very good position here, near me. As you can see its halfway between the water closets and the front door.'

I felt that he could see my eyes light up.

'That will be five hundred *dirhams*, (one hundred and fifty U.S. dollars),' declared Haj, sensing he was close to a deal.

Five hundred *dirhams*, it was most of the money in my pocket, but I had no choice. I hoped to get bail in the morning, so I needed my own space to sit, gather my thoughts and perhaps even get some sleep. For that I needed a well-positioned mattress.

'Done, sounds like a bargain!' I said and shook Haj's hand, intrigued that even in that darkest of places, good old supply and demand capitalism still flourished.

True to his word Haj haggled a mattress for me from another prisoner who was selling his to buy pain killers, and I slumped down on it.

My makeshift bed was blood-streaked and piss-stained, but I had no choice. It was my own safe island.

Mattress deal done I picked up my conversation with Haj.

'It seems pretty lawless in here,' I remarked.

'It is. Emirati guards don't come inside or patrol. They're too scared. We prisoners police ourselves,' said Haj.

My stomach tightened. I was locked in with hundreds of hardened criminals, some of them killers, and assorted crazies like the Palestinian. There were no guards. How could that be?

'He's the sheriff in Dodge,' said Haj, pointing to a man built like a four-hundred-pound gorilla.

'He's Abdul, an Emirati prisoner.'

The finger point from Haj was the man-mountain's cue to make himself known and, as he closed in, I noticed his broad forehead and chubby cheeks dripped with perspiration. His very snug-fitting, three-quarter-length *dishdasha* was stained beneath his armpits and across his crotch area.

But his size and grubbiness weren't his main distinguishing features. Abdul only had one functioning eye. His right one had been sewn up. Inmates nicknamed him: Cyclops.

'Ah, Briteesh man, welcome!' Cyclops roared during our first encounter.

His left eye stared me down; it had me mesmerised, it was unblinking, like a shark's.

Short on small talk, Cyclops cut to the chase.

'I can get you phone and anything else you want, but, you pay me fifty *dirhams* each time I help you, OK, Briteesh? Fifty *dirhams*, remember!' he bellowed.

Fifty *dirhams* was about fourteen bucks and I was in no mood for bargaining with a one-eyed thug. I simply nodded.

'Yes, sure, whatever you want.'

Cyclops had business elsewhere in Hotel Hell and, satisfied he'd marked my cards, he waddled off and left me to ponder how I was going to get some sleep.

Getting shut-eye amid the general din and fluorescent lights, which evidently burned day and night, wasn't easy.

I'd purloined a dirty blanket and tried to doze, but then an orderly prodded me with a plate of rubbery chicken and rice I'd requested many hours before. I waved him away. I wasn't hungry.

Just as my eyes closed again there was awful, unearthly cry.

'Come on, you bastard, come on!'

'I'm going to fucking kill you.'

Peeping from beneath my blanket, I recognised the man shouting death threats was Farid, the Egyptian I'd met earlier; no longer the placid, urbane businessman.

I could see he was already trading punches with a young Arab man who was obviously the aggressor, just a few feet away.

The battling duo edged closer, fists flying, and eventually one of them was stomping around on my mattress; I couldn't see who because I'd buried myself beneath my blanket and I was praying I wouldn't get hurt.

After a minute or so Farid's warrior cries, became moans of agony, then: silence.

I peeped out again. Farid was slumped on the floor in a heap. He'd been stabbed and his back slashed with a make-shift knife made from a toothbrush and two razor blades; the blades had been pushed into the melted end of the toothbrush.

The young Arab had abandoned his weapon and had already staggered away as bright, fresh, crimson blood, oozed from Farid's body and seeped toward my mattress.

Inmates who'd watched and cheered on the bloody brawl to its gory end, stepped forward and heaved Farid over their shoulders to carry him off to who knew where? They were like 'seconds' in a prize fight.

'Fat chance of him getting any medical help,' I said under my breath. At the same time, I thought about Farid's wife and kids.

Within minutes the chamber returned to normality, as if nothing had happened, and I never saw Farid again or found out whether he'd survived. I sincerely hoped he had.

For the rest of the night I laid on my mattress, thanking God I'd suffered no harm and reflecting on what had been the worst day of my life.

Only hours before I'd been in a luxury hotel, living it large, going about my normal business of making money like thousands of other expats. Whatever problem, the Emirates pilots had with me, I didn't deserve to end up like this. Yes, they'd lost their shirts; their life savings in some cases; but I had plans to refinance the deal and to compensate them.

Then, what would Susan, my wife, be thinking? She'd be at home worried sick because the office would have let her know I'd been arrested.

My mind was still racing as I did my best to get some sleep, already realising hope of freedom is the only true asset any prisoner has.

'Peter, you need to get a grip. Adapt to survive.' I told myself, as I stiffened my resolve to face whatever the next day might bring.

'Come on,' I muttered. 'You're Peter Margetts, a fit, forty-six-year-old and a self-made millionaire who's pulled himself up by his bootstraps from nothing.'

'You've come from nowhere, survived career ups and downs. You're as at home mixing with high-flyers on Dubai's golf courses and smart cocktail parties as you are downing a pint with the hoi polloi.'

'You've got loyal company staff and loving wife and beautiful daughter who need you back home.'

Personal pep talk over, I was calmer. I willed myself to sleep.

But looking back I could never have foreseen, not in my wildest imaginings, that first night of incarceration in violent Al Rashidiya was just the beginning of an horrendous prison ordeal that would cost me my marriage, my mental and physical health, and almost, my life.

A new dawn broke suddenly over Al Rashidiya, as it always does in the Gulf, and I was woken from a fitful sleep by fractious inmates stumbling clumsily over each other and their mattresses, clutching ragged towels and slivers of soap, to join the growing lines for the latrines. One or two farted unselfconsciously as they swaggered past me.

I needed a pee, but I couldn't face it and decided to hold out until the crowd thinned.

Despite the horror of Farid's stabbing the previous night I'd been able to grab a couple of hours sleep and I'd cheered myself enough to be confident I'd get bail and be set free. More importantly, I was looking forward to being reunited with my precious wife, Susan, and daughter Olivia later that day.

Because this was all a terrible mistake, wasn't it? I'd been locked up in error and someone was going to get me out today… right?

Just as I was thinking about hiring lawyers and working out how best to scrape bail money together, there was a massive crash of metal on wood.

I spun round to see Cyclops had dumped a huge vat of *fool* on a trestle table. It was breakfast time.

Dear reader, for those of you who don't know, *fool* is the Arabic name for *fava* beans. *Fool* is the sibling of a better known Middle Eastern delicacy *humous,* but unlike *humous, fool* has never quite made it to the international culinary hall of fame.

And easy to see why; *fool* has a gooey texture and an off-putting dark brown color. OK, I'll say it: even *fool's* greatest fans must admit; it looks like runny shit.

The metallic crunch of a cauldron of *fool* on the table was the starting gun for hundreds of inmates clutching aluminum plates to rush forward to begin fighting man-to-man for a plateful of Cyclop's signature dish. With no spoons, or cutlery, they dived in and scooped it up with bare fingers. Feeding time at the zoo would have been more orderly.

Although I was very hungry, I had no stomach for a plate of *fool*; I needed my strength for the day ahead, but I wasn't ready to pitch into the melee.

Just I was gazing at the seething mass gobbling down breakfast, a guard opened the main gate and bellowed: 'Peter Nicholas, Peter Nicholas, come to gate please.'

'This was it?' I thought, 'It's freedom time, they're letting me go.'

My actual surname, Margetts, just hadn't registered with

Dubai's officialdom, but in my desperate circumstances they could call me anything. Peter Nicholas was just fine.

'Follow me please,' the guard ordered and escorted me through the main metal door on to the first-floor landing.

I hadn't been prepared though for what awaited me on the other side of the door.

To my shock and utter joy it was my wife, Susan, and business partner, Kieran.

I must have looked disheveled in shirt sleeves and suit trousers, eyes red from lack of sleep and emotionally exhausted. God knows what the pair of them thought when they saw me.

'You've come to take me home,' I gasped.

Susan was a strong character and during our entire relationship I saw her cry perhaps only once or twice, but as I stood in the doorway she broke down in tears; Kieran too.

I fell into Susan's embrace and hugged her like never before, my face buried in the tresses of her soft blonde hair. I drew huge mental strength from the warmth of her body and the smell of her familiar cologne. At that moment I couldn't hold my emotions and I cried.

'Behind that metal door, where I've just come from, is a horror story you wouldn't believe,' I whispered to Susan.

'If I don't get free from here, I don't think I can get through this, my love.'

Susan was in pieces and held me tighter; her lovely blue eyes closed; our heads rested together.

As we comforted each other I turned to Kieran and asked if he'd contacted my lawyer Ludmilla Yamalova.

'Did you tell Ludmilla I'd been arrested?'

'Yes,' said Kieran. 'But Ludmilla said she can't help you

because she is a civil lawyer. She said you needed a criminal lawyer.'

'But, don't worry, that's been organised.

'I've got a criminal brief lined up for you, Peter. He wanted U.S.$30,000 up front.'

Thirty grand was about the last money in our corporate account.

'OK pay him, I've got to get out of here,' I said to Kieran, happier in the knowledge I had a lawyer working on my case.

I was fumbling through a bag of clean socks, shirts and pants Susan had brought me when another shocking episode unfolded.

Just as the three of us huddled together, a tall, heavy-set Arab prisoner staggered out of the main door of the chamber behind us carrying a lifeless young man in T-shirt and jeans in his muscled arms.

With little ceremony, or real care, he dumped the male victim at the feet of, Susan, Kieran, me, and guards, who'd been detailed to keep an eye on us.

Something hit me. I immediately recognised the body on the floor as the youth who'd attacked Farid, the Egyptian businessman, the night before. He looked dead to me.

The guards stood motionless, just staring, but the tall Arab sprang into action and grabbed a newspaper Susan had brought me. He rolled it up and shoved it down the lifeless young man's throat.

If his intention was to create an airway and save the young man's life, it didn't work. After a minute or so there was no sign of him breathing; no pulse, nothing.

A reluctant senior guard then grudgingly bent down and

wiped his fingers across the young man's chest; detached, airily, like he was brushing dust off a piece of furniture.

Then he rattled something off in Arabic to his colleagues and turned to me, Susan and Kieran: 'This man's finished. He's dead. Too much drugs.'

I wondered if the dead man had been high on drugs when he stabbed Farid in the back the night before?

The guards' coldness toward giving first-aid told me that the sudden death of an inmate was not unusual at Al Rashidiya. However, the appearance of a stiff on the landing, on their watch suddenly sent them into a frenzy of shouting and waving arms at each other.

In fact, there was so much gesticulating and chaotic rushing around that, to be frank, had Susan and Kieran and myself nipped down the open back stairs and scarpered from Al Rashidiya, none of them would have noticed we'd gone.

The thought of doing a runner crossed my mind for a few seconds, but I told myself: 'Steady on, Peter, they'll almost certainly catch you and you'll be put away forever.'

After some minutes the deceased young Arab had been stretchered to Al Rashidiya's morgue and the agitated guards had calmed down a little, enough to turn their attention back to us.

'*Yellah, yellah,* you leave now,' they shouted at Susan and Kieran.

As the guards shoved me back through the chamber door and started closing it, I yelled:

'Susan, leave Dubai, my love. Take Olivia. Get on a flight to London, I beg you.'

Tears trickled down Susan's face, but she managed a weak

smile back and nodded.

'And Kieran, for fuck sake, bust the lawyer's balls. I need to get out of here,' I screamed, realising I was going to spend another day and night in Al Rashidiya.

Kieran gave me a confident thumbs-up; the pair were gone, and the steel gate had slammed shut.

Back in the chamber, I fell down on my mattress, close to my new companion, Haj. I was still in shock from what I'd witnessed on the landing and began to fear what other horrors lay ahead.

Barely a few minutes passed before an inmate, deep inside the massed ranks of other prisoners, rose to his feet, tilted his head back and let out an almighty and highly emotive:

'*Allahu Akbar!*'

He repeated this three times.

Instantly, the chamber was gripped in silence. En-masse, 400 prisoners dropped to their knees in the prostrate Muslim prayer position; a point of visual high drama and an incredibly profound moment when it happened.

'Haj, what's going on?' I whispered.

'They're about to pray for the soul of the guy who just died,' he murmured.

The ceremony, which involved orations from the Koran, lasted thirty minutes and afterward a quietness, like a calming, air-blown caress, settled on the chamber. Inmates remained immersed in somber thoughts, until the morning.

The death of one of their own had clearly moved them.

So, there was a scrap of humanity in the jungle after all.

2

The Mad Hatter's Tea Party

Next morning, I got a message from guards I was being bussed to court and I should get ready.

'This was it,' I thought to myself, 'I'll get bail and get out of this menagerie for good.'

'Maybe I'd be freed in time to get on the same evening flight to London as my wife Susan and our daughter Olivia?'

I'd also got word through the guards that my office had engaged the hot-shot, criminal defence lawyer, Kieran mentioned during his visit. My new brief had been paid his outrageous U.S.$30,000 fee upfront.

I didn't know his name. I guessed he'd make himself known to me when I got to court, where all he had to do was convince the judge: Peter Margetts, prominent Dubai entrepreneur, all-round, good guy, was an honest property developer, not a fraudster, who ought to be released immediately. Not only because his wife and kid needed him, but if the Emirates pilots wanted their investment back, his client could only work on a financial rescue package if he was free and not in jail. Didn't those lines of argument make sense?

I thought so, that's why my tail was up as I started shoving a few clothes and toiletries in a plastic bag to take with me to court.

Haj leaned across and told me:

'Mr. Peter, ask the judge for *kafala*. Remember that word my friend: *kafala, kaar-faar-laah*! It's Arabic for bail. Keep saying *kafala, kafala* to the judge, don't forget!'

'*Kaar-faar-laah,*' I repeated dramatically, 'I'm sure my lawyer will ask for bail for me but, I got it, thanks Haj.'

'And good luck to you,' smiled the kindly Iranian, as I was handcuffed with fifty other prisoners and herded on to a jail bus, similar to the ones American kids are bussed into school in, only with bars on the window.

'Where are we going?' I asked a guard.

'We're taking you to the Court of Misdemeanors.'

'Court of Misdemeanors?' I repeated, checking I'd heard correctly. It sounded like a name from medieval England.

As the bus bounced along, I glanced at the blank faces of other prisoners, a mix of Arabs and Asian men, young and old. None spoke; they just stared blankly out of the windows at commuters on the E44 highway and the bleak industrial zone we trundled through.

What were their crimes, I wondered? Murder, drugs, rape? Perhaps it was something like: kissing a girlfriend in public?

Or, were they like me respectable property developers caught up in the fall-out from Dubai's poisonous checks laws?

There was only one way to find out.

The man sitting next to me turned out to be Bassam, a Bahraini; very slight built, perhaps a 110 pounds at most.

Bassam was charming; he spoke English as well as any UK native and revealed that his wife was a dentist in Marylebone, a district of London I knew well. Funny old world, I thought.

As we chatted away like long-lost friends, but, handcuffed

and bumping around on a bus like dried-peas in a tin can, I found it amusing to think Bassam's wife was likely to be stuck in London's West End traffic ahead of a nice day drilling teeth!

Bassam told me he was a property developer who, like me, had signed dozens of post-dated security checks which to that bounced after Dubai's financial crash. Like me, he'd been arrested at work and hauled off to the hellhole known as Al Rashidiya.

As Bassam and I got deeper into conversation, a curly-haired, bearded, young Arab, sitting opposite, decided to lean in and listen. He said he was Syrian.

More to be polite than anything else I asked him,

'And what were you arrested for, matey?'

'I was in fight with a friend. I stab him, I kill him,' he said very matter-of-factly.

As Bassam and I mentally absorbed in silence what we'd just heard, the Syrian went on,: 'Why you guys picked up?'

In unison we said: 'Bounced checks'

The killer's dark eyes sparkled with amusement: 'Ha, ha!' he chortled. 'I'll be out of jail before you two!'

Both Bassam and I smiled back, hesitant to believe what he'd just said.

No, no, no, he's wrong, I thought to myself. I'm not going to jail for longer than a murderer. Besides, my lawyer's going to get me freed today.

'Ignore him, he's an idiot!' Bassam, reassured me.

Thirty minutes later the bus pulled up at the Court of Misdemeanors in the main Dubai courts building overlooking Dubai Creek. It's a massive 1970s 'mashup', from an era when the city-state began the first phase of its transformation from dusty, desert town to space-age metropolis.

The fifty of us, still handcuffed, were herded off the bus to an underground dungeon beneath the courts where we were pushed toward huge cages packed to bursting with men, women and children, like animals in an unruly zoo.

The heat, noise and stench from so many sweaty humans was overwhelming.

I was the only Westerner in the massive men's cage and I thought my white face would make it easier for my lawyer to find me for a pre-hearing chat. But, as the minutes and hours ticked by and other prisoners began to move upstairs to court, there was no sign of my own 'Rumpole of the Bailey'!

As I sweated in the stifling heat, wondering what the hell was going on, a couple of guys pushed their way through the mob toward me. From the state of their giddiness and glassy eyes, they were obviously on a drug trip.

The older one, an Emirati, grey-haired, in his forties with a large, beaked nose, reminded me of Gonzo from The Muppets.

His pal, or perhaps his boyfriend, was Russian in his early twenties, dark-haired, with a crew cut. He packed the kind of tattooed, muscled arms and chest that were only built on steroids.

The young Russian's eyes bulged and from time to time he jabbed his massive fists at nobody in particular, shadow boxing an invisible opponent.

Although both were as high as kites, the Emirati was vaguely coherent and spoke good English, although I wasn't convinced that, in his 'trippy' state, he understood he was about to appear before a judge.

'You two look like you've been smoking a crack pipe,' I

said half-jokingly.

'Yes, you're right,' giggled Salman, the Emirati. 'We have, can we get you something?'

'Err, no thanks, I'm up in court shortly.'

One thing puzzled me. The 'odd couple' had been held at a police station until that morning, so how come they were high?

'How did you get a drug fix when you've been in police custody?' I asked

'Oh, it's easy, we bribe the police,' said Salman. 'No problem, *mafi-mushkela.*'

'You can bribe almost any cop in Dubai everyone knows that, it's part of life.'

Salman's explanation solved the conundrum of why so many inmates were tripping at my digs at Al Rashidiya. The police and guards clearly supplemented their modest salaries with a bit of dealing.

'How much do you spend on drugs, Salman?'

'My family are very wealthy; I get an allowance, about U.S.$25,000 a month, so I have enough to buy what I need, crack, charlie, brown sugar, E, spice, whatever.'

The pair of drugged clowns quickly tired of me and my intrusive questions and wandered off to pester someone else, leaving me to mull over Dubai; the land of contradictions and aching hypocrisy.

Officially, there was zero tolerance of drugs. The punishment for dealing was the death penalty. And yet, if Salman's story was true, corrupt local forces of law and order were an integral part of what was obviously a thriving underground drugs scene.

I hadn't asked what the pair were charged with, but, if Salman was a member of a prominent Emirati family, I knew he'd spend little time behind bars, if he was convicted at all. The elders in his family might even pull a few strings to ensure his friend, the Russian, wasn't deported. Such is the way the local Emirati population deal with their own black sheep.

But I digress.

The basement tannoy crackled into life.

'Peter Nicholas, Peter Nicholas,' cried a disjointed voice.

Showtime, I was on!

Guards led me handcuffed from the underground cages upstairs to a maze of noisy, chaotic corridors where I joined a confusion of prisoners, their families, Emirati lawyers and their clerks, all shouting at each other and gesticulating like they were guests at The Mad Hatter's Tea Party.

As I was bundled toward court five, I felt hopelessly under-dressed for the occasion: unkept, hair-in-a-mess, unshaven in tracksuit bottoms and a creased, grubby shirt. Not the perfect look for any court appearance, but hey-ho! there was nothing I could do.

In court I found myself among a gaggle of lawyers, their clients and court officials and, to my alarm, I discovered my case had started without me in shouty Arabic with the prosecutor verbally batting back and forth while a short-tempered Emirati judge sat on high in black robes with a bright yellow sash.

When I made myself known, both judge and prosecutor paused and glared at me as if I was a nuisance.

'Mr. Margetts, what a cheek for turning up for your own trial!' I imagined their thoughts.

But, where the freaking hell, was my lawyer?

Cue: Omar, the man to whom the office had paid a hefty thirty grand. He'd been loitering at the back of the court all the time.

As the judge and prosecutor continued their shouting match as if I wasn't even there: 'Mr. Peter, hello, I'm Omar, I'm representing you today,' he grinned.

Omar was an Emirati, in his thirties, plump, dressed in a traditional white *dishdasha* and headdress. He seemed a pleasant enough chap. But, he held no papers or files about my case, no briefcase or indeed any of the accoutrements you'd expect an attorney to carry, not even a notepad and pen.

His demeanor reminded me of a smiling waiter offering canapés at an ambassador's cocktail party.

At that point I'd still no idea what I'd been charged with, what my defense was, and more importantly: how about getting me bail?

'Nice to meet you Omar; are we going to discuss my case? I need to get bail today.' I said expectantly.

Omar didn't enlighten me. Instead, to my absolute consternation, he stepped forward and joined the argument with the judge and prosecutor in rapid-fire Arabic.

I didn't understand why they were yelling so aggressively, although I heard the name Peter Nicholas mentioned several times.

This is not going to end well, I thought.

After a minute or so the shouting subsided and then, for a few moments, the judge looked me up and down.

I stared back from in the middle of the courtroom, ragged, grubby, wide-eyed, like a middle-aged Oliver Twist asking for more.

Without a word to me the care-worn judge just sighed and dismissed me disdainfully with a deft hand-wave, like a crabby old duke signaling his footman to fuck off.

The court clerk shouted for the next case, and it was all over.

As guards swarmed in to take me away, I spun around to my brief: 'What just happened Omar?'

'Don't worry, Mr. Peter, I'll speak to you later,' he exclaimed, heading for the exit.

'By the way, here's my business card my friend. Give me a call.'

'Good-bye, Mr. Peter; good luck!'

A swirl of his *dishdasha*, and the March Hare skipped away from the tea-party and vanished in the teeming court corridors; I, meanwhile, was bustled by guards down to the underground dungeon from whence I came no more than ten minutes before.

The feeling of utter despair weighed on me like a ton of lead.

That court appearance was supposed to have been my get-out-of jail card. But what happened to my bail application? And why had I paid a legal shyster U.S.$30,000 to do absolutely zippo?

I was still in deep shock when I noticed guards were marching me to a waiting bus, already almost full of Arab and Asian prisoners.

It was similar to the bus that had brought me to court, but not the same one.

Once aboard and seated I turned to a young Arab prisoner, and asked: 'What's happening? Where are we going? This isn't the bus I came on.'

'That's right,' he said. 'This bus take you jail.'

'Fuck!'

'This is all a big mistake. I'm not going to jail.'

'Sorry, friend; judge say you guilty. He sent you jail.'

'Found guilty? Guilty of what?'

'And prison? How long for?' I asked him.

The Arab prisoner could only shrug. Of course. he didn't know.

A half-hour later the bus swept through gates in a twenty-five-feet-high wall, topped with razor wire, as we rode into the big-house, the horror prison I'd already heard very bad things about: Dubai Central.

In a reception area called quarantine, guards ordered me and hundreds of other prisoners to strip to our underwear.

Then, they handed us Chairman Mao-style prison pyjamas.

Each had different colored stripes: blue, red, white or green.

The one they ordered me to put on was white with a blue stripe.

'What do the different colors mean?' I asked one of the guards

'Blue stripe means you've been sentenced to between one and three years,' he said casually.

For several moments I was utterly dumbstruck, my knees weakened, my stomach clenched, and I could hardly breathe.

'Welcome to Dubai Central, Mr. Peter.'

3

When did it all go wrong?

You're probably wondering how a worldly, expatriate executive lacked enough savvy to steer clear of jail in Dubai?

And just how did Dubai's 2008 economic meltdown result in me being jailed?

It all began in December 1963 at London's world-renowned Great Ormond Street Hospital.

I wasn't born there.

I was left on the steps by my birth mother who walked off into the night.

Why she abandoned me, wrapped in a blanket in a Moses basket on a cold, winter evening in London, remains a mystery to this day.

Five years later I was reminded I'd been an abandoned baby when I was admitted to Great Ormond Street on the edict of my loving, adoptive parents for an operation to have my sticky-out ears pinned back.

Afterwards, I sat alone on my hospital bed looking like a little-boy-lost, when a cheerful Scottish nurse popped in and started to chat, I guess to lift my spirits a bit and to talk about me going home.

I can see her now. She was in her late twenties. She had a perfect oval face framed by long, glossy, raven-hair.

We'd been through the gossipy, mundane stuff.

'Where were you born?' and 'Do you have a mum and dad?'

I told her I'd been adopted and had fantastic, adoptive parents.

For some reason the curious nurse scuttled off to check my hospital records. When she returned to my bedside her face was all smiles.

'My God Peter, you're the little boy I remember being left on the steps outside years ago!' she exclaimed.

'All the nurses wondered what happened to you.'

'Now, you're back!'

To be frank, to a five-year-old lad who was still in pain from having his ears pinned back, the nurse's realization that I'd been an abandoned baby meant more to her than it did to me.

My adoptive dad, Ken Margetts, and mom, Aida, had rescued me from an orphanage when I was a few months old and the fact I'd been abandoned by my birth mother on the steps of a hospital had never been deeply discussed around the breakfast table when I was growing up. So, I probably reacted to the nurse's surprise with a shrug and a request for another glass of milk and more biscuits.

I'd been a happy kid growing up, partly because my dad, Ken, was such great guy and role model.

He'd served in the British Army during World War Two and he had been based in Aden, Yemen, then a key UK wartime base. By chance, whilst on leave in Istanbul, Turkey, he spotted my mom, Aida, in Taksim Square, taking in the evening air with her extended Armenian family.

Long story short: dad boldly introduced himself to Aida, it was 'love-at-first-sight', they married and soon after V.E.

Day they settled in the southern English seaside town of Southend-On-Sea.

My mom and dad couldn't have children of their own and, besides me, they also adopted my brother, Joseph, my senior by six years, and my sister, Magda, who was four years older.

After leaving the Army dad became a civil servant at the UK's Ministry of Defence and, although I can never remember us having a lot of money, as kids we wanted for nothing.

My treasured childhood memories included hot summers and wonderful holidays at my parents' rented caravan in the English south coast town of Selsey, where, with the encouragement of my keen cyclist dad, I developed a love of open countryside and sports of all kinds, especially football.

Due to dad's job we moved home a few times. When I was eight my parents bought a house in Hounslow, a suburb in north west London, where I attended a Catholic comprehensive school, St. Mark's.

To my surprise my teachers saw some spark of intelligence in me and encouraged me to work hard, but I was more interested in sports and chasing girls. I left school with five minor qualifications, what were then called CSE's.

On my last day at St Mark's, form teacher Miss Winter remarked with uncanny accuracy:

'Peter Margetts, you're either going to be a millionaire or end up in jail, I don't know which!'

Miss Winter, as it turned out, you were right on both counts!

When I left school, aged sixteen, I didn't know what I wanted to do with my life. First, I became an apprentice bricklayer, building the foundations of London's Canary Wharf financial center, an iconic and towering symbol of capitalism; one of Prime Minister Margaret Thatcher's successful legacies.

I then took my bricklaying skills to Leeds, a northern English city, where I was already a keen supporter of Leeds United, the local football club.

Friends used to ask me, a southerner, why I supported Leeds United, a team 200 miles from where I came from?

The story I told them was that my brother Joe, and I had been watching Leeds play Chelsea in the 1970 Cup Final competition. I'd asked Joe who he was supporting and he'd said, 'Chelsea.'

'Then I'm supporting Leeds,' I said, and from that day I became a passionate, lifelong fan.

Looking back on my early career I pissed my life away until my late twenties. I drank vast amounts of alcohol in night and day binges with friends. I also indulged in drugs; at first, nothing harmful, but eventually spliff joints gave way to hard drugs like cocaine. Whatever I earned I spent. All my wages disappeared on a hedonistic lifestyle of booze, drugs and women.

During those wasted years, aged eighteen, I took off with some other lads to work in construction in the Spanish holiday playground of Benidorm. Then, we moved to Gibraltar, a British enclave, on the southern tip of the Iberian peninsular known universally as 'Gib.'

One night, myself and a British pal called Steve, who was around my age, with a huge head of curly ginger hair, were both pissed as farts in a Gib pub where we met a jolly German called Werner.

Likeable Werner was a dry-witted, middle-aged used-car salesman and UK readers will know immediately what I mean when I say he was the German version of Arthur Daley.

Arthur, as Brits will know, was a much loved fictional character in a hit TV series "Minder" played beautifully by the late George Cole.

Werner perfectly fitted the show's publicity blurb about the fictional Arthur Daley: 'A socially ambitious, but highly unscrupulous importer-exporter, a wholesaler, a used-car salesman and purveyor of anything else from which there was money to be made, whether within the law or not.'

That was Werner to a Tee.

In the early hours, when the bar was about to close, Werner revealed he had a forty-foot sailing yacht, in the harbor and he was casting off the next day on the first leg of a round-the-world-voyage. Would Steve and I like to be the crew?

Ordering another round of beers, naturally, we said, 'Fuck, yes.'

Still hammered on booze and wobbly with excitement Steve and I went back to our apartments, stuffed our few clothes and possessions into suitcases and sailed at dawn with Werner out of Gibraltar harbor. Our destination, the Spanish Atlantic islands of Gran Canaria, seven hundred nautical miles away, or seven days sailing.

I wish I could remember the name of the boat, but it's too long ago.

I was still semi-conscious on a bunk below deck, but beginning to come around from my drunken stupor as we slipped through the Straits of Gibraltar with the Moroccan coast to port.

My head thumped and I felt like I'd been press-ganged; the eighteenth-century British Navy practice of dragging drunken young men out of pubs on the English south coast and forcing them into service on warships.

'Come on, you two,' cried an ebullient Werner, sporting a Hawaiian shirt and brandishing a bottle of schnapps.

'Let's drink to King Neptune!'

'King who? Fuck me, no more alcohol,' I muttered, as the growing sea swell made my nausea worse.

I was able to find a porthole and threw up, which helped.

Now, I should point out, my pal Steve was from Great Yarmouth, a seaside town in eastern England, and he'd been on the briny before, but the closest I'd been to sailing was with a girlfriend in a rowing boat on London's Serpentine lake.

To be fair Werner made allowances for my lack of maritime expertise. Putting down the schnapps bottle, for a moment he declared: 'Peter, it's OK. You can sleep now, I've put you on nightwatch.'

'Oh jeez, thanks.'

And so, we three-men-in-a-boat sailed on, narrowly missing reefs off the island of Madeira on the third day.

I quickly realized, I was never going to truly find my sea legs, that said, I quite enjoyed night watch.

Werner slapped the yacht into autopilot mode and my job was to simply stay awake and make sure we didn't hit anything. This was easier said than done because our dodgy radar flickered intermittently, and the rolling Atlantic Ocean ahead was just a velvet blackness apart from the reflection of a myriad twinkling stars and lights from distant ships.

It was about three a.m. on the fourth night and Werner and Steve were sleeping below deck. I was up top, contemplating the meaning of life, on night watch, when there was a sudden, massive blast from a ship's horn, and I mean massive. The bellowing noise was eardrum shattering and scared me shitless.

'Fuck me! what the hell is that?'

It blasted again, and again, so loud the sound vibrations made my teeth chatter.

Then from the darkness on my right loomed the mountainous shape of a supertanker, so close that the sea wash from its huge, bulbous bow cascaded across ours. You will understand when I say I nearly shat my pants.

Paralysed by fear, I whispered a silent prayer and then gaped, open-mouthed, as its huge, barnacled hull sliced through the pitch-black seas to my right, almost within touching distance, Its giant superstructure was like a seagoing skyscraper.

King Neptune must have been looking down because within seconds the marine behemoth slid by, missing us, but only just. A few feet or so nearer and it would have crushed Werner's yacht into thousands of splinters and sent us down to 'Davy Jones's locker.'

My heart was still thumping like a terrified rabbit's when bleary-eyed Werner and Steve stumbled up to the main deck, for a collective,

'What the fuck?'

The maritime monster's stern vanished into the darkness from whence it came, all three of us decided, another drink!

My first sea adventure wasn't over. On the fifth day a squall blew up and waves became mountainous, but we ploughed on to Gran Canaria.

I took comfort from Werner's general air of confidence we'd make it, even though winds howled, and Atlantic waves crashed around us.

'Don't worry, guys, this boat is strong, this is nothing!' He cried.

The boat's rolling motion made my seasickness worse and I spent much of my remaining night-watches groaning in a corner and throwing up over the side.

Being unsuited to the sea's motion and nearly being crushed by a supertanker made me realize life on the open ocean was not for me, and no one was more pleased when the Gran Canaria port of Pasito Blanco hove into view.

The next port of call on Werner's epic sea odyssey was set to be Dakar, Senegal, followed by a twenty-one-day transatlantic crossing to Rio De Janeiro, Brazil. To finance that voyage, our enthusiastic captain said he must return to Germany to sell more cars!

I'd already made my mind up to abandon ship and, happy to be on *terra firma* instead of a swaying deck, I said a reluctant goodbye to Werner and found myself a job at the Holiday Bar in the resort of Playa de las Americas working as a barker, cajoling mostly German and Scandinavian punters to step inside with the lure a free cocktail.

For the first time, I realised I was a good at selling and, within a week, the Holiday Bar was heaving with new customers. I remember my delight at earning U.S.$60 a day in cash, a lot of money in 1983.

But, much as I loved the Holiday Bar job, it was seasonal. When I returned to the UK, I dated a Northern Irish girl called Linda, who one day said: 'Peter, what are you doing with your life?'

That was, as they say nowadays, a light bulb moment, and I decided to improve myself.

I enrolled at Brighton College of Technology to study for an ONC qualification. From there, I was fortunate enough to be accepted by Liverpool University, where I gained an honors degree in Building Management and Technology.

But the job in Playa de Las Americas had taught me sales was my *forte* and with my Liverpool degree I found a job with the Co-operative Society financial services arm, selling investments like pension plans to Co-op customers.

My wild, hedonistic days were finally put behind me when I was 'cold called' by a recruitment firm and landed a job at an American stockbroking firm, which, ironically, installed me at London's Canary Wharf, the massive financial center I'd help build as a bricklayer!

From there I moved to one of the world's biggest financial services firm, Towry Law, based in Kuala Lumpur in Malaysia.

Fast forward again, and I joined three close business associates to form the Clearwater partnership. My new base? Singapore.

The dynamic island-state was rapidly expanding its infrastructure to match rival Hong Kong. Highways, shopping malls, skyscrapers sprang up, seemingly, overnight.

Crucially for me though, Singapore was packed with expatriate workers on generous remuneration packages with nowhere to invest their low-tax earnings. I knew I could help them find a home in exchange for their spare cash!

Singapore was a financial services salesman's dream and in 2003, aged forty, I made my first big money; a commission of U.S.$300,000 on a U.S.$12 million investment.

Making that kind of windfall was a significant moment for a man who'd once been a piss artist and spent every buck he'd earned.

For the first time I felt rich and my bank account showed a massive credit. I wasn't going to wipe it out with nights on the town, women and drugs, as I'd done so many times before.

Fatefully, at the same time, my wife-to-be, Susan, also entered the picture.

I'd known Susan as a platonic friend since St. Mark's comprehensive school, where she was also a pupil. After our teens we'd lost touch, but I learned she was working for a marketing firm in Dubai.

By pure serendipity, Susan paid a brief visit to Malaysia, we had dinner together and a romantic spark kindled.

I'd found her effortlessly attractive with blonde hair and ready smile. When she returned to Dubai, I decided to join her; we set up home together as a couple in December 2004.

It was a joyous, optimistic time; I'd put the wasted years behind me, and I couldn't have been happier.

Little did I know, the move to Dubai was the beginning of my life's darkest chapter.

I had no job lined up in Dubai, so, using a friend's connection I found a berth as a salesman with Imagine Homes run by UK celebrity property tycoon Grant Bovey, better known in Britain as the former husband of television presenter Anthea Turner.

Hugely ambitious, Bovey was attempting to expand his 'buy-to-let' empire with a unique business model. Imagine bought blocks of flats in the UK, about a year from completion. The company then sold eighty percent of the flats to 'buy-to-let' investors, with a guaranteed seven and a half percent yield. Meanwhile, Imagine, bought the remaining twenty percent using a bank loan. It was an untried *modus operandi,* and Bovey believed he'd nailed a money spinner.

Half of Imagine's investors came from overseas, so, being based in Dubai among expats with plenty of tax-free cash to invest, I was a natural shoo-in to sell Bovey's homes for him.

I was a star salesman and shifted almost 200 properties in the first year, earning myself a total commission of U.S.$500,000.

Flushed with success, I wanted a bigger slice of the pie, and I approached Bovey to ask if he'd make me a partner. He wasn't interested.

Around then the UK property market was showing signs of slowing, especially the 'buy-to-let' sector. But Dubai was still booming, so it was an easy decision for me to leave Imagine and set up my own property development company.

I dreamed up the name 'Hampstead and Mayfair Ltd,' by picking the names of two smart areas of London. I thought investors would think there was a company with a great ring to it. I was open for business!

The word soaraway doesn't begin to describe the dynamic Dubai property market. It was on fire!

Back in 2002, Dubai's Ruler, Sheikh Mohammed bin Rashid Al-Maktoum, had made the market changing decision that foreigners could buy and actually own property in the city-state. It was a seminal moment in Dubai's history that prompted a *tsunami* of foreign cash, and I mean many billions of dollars.

Thousands of potential investors poured in from Moscow, Beijing, London and New York with a deposit tucked in their back pockets and their heads fixed on making a financial killing. They were, mostly, buying 'off-plan, sight unseen,' and, they didn't care as long as they got a toe-hold in the property market, which was so hot, so manic, hundreds of foreign buyers would rock up at every new apartment block launch.

Sky-rocketing prices meant investors could 'flip' an apartment within hours, not days, for a fat profit. Buy at breakfast, market it at lunchtime and sell over dinner, was not unknown.

Construction firms, like state-owned Emaar, were even forced to keep launch chaos to a manageable level by holding a lottery beforehand, with only those holding a winning ticket able to put in a bid for a new villa or apartment.

At the time I remember thinking Dubai's property market was like being aboard a runaway train packed with passengers pissed on champagne, but with no one in the caboose at the back to pull on the brakes. It was bound to hurtle off the tracks at some point down the line, I think we all knew that, but nobody knew when. Meanwhile, profits were, absolutely astronomic, and I wanted in on the action, so did investors.

The first project of Hampstead and Mayfair's, was construction of a couple of villas in upmarket Jumeirah, a millionaires' playground with white sandy beaches, luxury hotels and apartments stretching south to the iconic Palm development.

The property industry was still white-hot and my first clients were six Emirates pilots. The flyers were high earners, in tax-free, Klondike Dubai, with lots of spare cash looking for a home and they invested a total of U.S.$1 million.

The stunning new properties were built in short order and the pilots got their investment back plus the guaranteed thirty percent profit, as I'd promised them.

My company also made U.S.$1 million on the deal, and bingo! Hampstead and Mayfair was off and running. Thank you very much.

Pilots are big gossips and word soon got around the Dubai-based airline that Peter Margetts's Hampstead and Mayfair was a winner. And forty-two Emirates pilots decided they too wanted to give the Dubai property roulette wheel a spin, this time for a cumulative investment of U.S.$7 million.

The deal was this: they loaned me U.S.$7 million to buy the land and build the apartments known as The Waterfront, and within six months of their investment they could sell for their original outlay, plus a guaranteed thirty percent profit.

So, typically a pilot who'd invested say U.S.$400,000 could confidently expect to sell his apartment in the soaring market for at least U.S.$490,000, 'pocketing' a handy U.S.$90,000. Happy days!

As was the business norm in Dubai, I gave the forty-two pilots post-dated security checks, signed by me as CEO of Hampstead and Mayfair, to the value of their investment plus one-third profit. Then, we sat back to watch the new Waterfront apartment block rise out of the sand and dreamt of how we'd spend our expected windfall.

Fatefully, the pilots and I had failed to heed or appreciate the economic danger signs already flashing in faraway America.

As 2008 unfolded, the sub-prime mortgage scandal had already spawned fears of another Great Depression similar to the one that followed the 1929 Wall Street Crash. Tottering Lehman Brothers bank had yet to collapse, but the global credit crunch was well underway.

Meanwhile in the UK lines of worried customers had gathered outside branches of Northern Rock, the first run on a British high street bank since the 1860s.

We'd started to notice the warning signs, but whether it was because we lived in a bubble in swaggeringly, confident Dubai I don't know, but everyone, including me, believed the United Arab Emirates would escape financial meltdown, and if the worst happened, and the market crashed, we could bank on Dubai's Ruler, Sheikh Mohammed, stepping in with a bailout.

What transpired was beyond our worst imagining.

By mid-2008, around the time of the pilots' U.S.$7 million loan to my firm, falling global economies threw a massive bucket of ice water on the city-state's already hugely over-heated property market. A dip in oil prices also added to the pressure.

It was such an almighty drenching there was nothing even the all-powerful and fabulously wealthy Sheikh Mo. could do to stop property values collapsing by at least fifty percent virtually overnight

Billions were wiped off Dubai's Stock Exchange, which plummeted seventy percent.

A massive flight of capital from Dubai meant construction projects worth half a trillion U.S. dollars were scrapped and thousands of workers were laid off.

The forest of cranes which to that had dominated Dubai's skyline for so long suddenly stopped turning because the, 'state-owned,' big three developers: Emaar, Nakheel and Dubai Holding, being responsible for seventy percent of Dubai's construction, were in danger of going bust.

Even saying those words would have been unthinkable in early 2008.

'Nakheel, part of the mega-wealthy Dubai Government in trouble? You're surely having a laugh.'

But it was horribly true.

After the Dubai property market collapsed you couldn't give apartments away. Scared investors began pulling out the property market big time and buyers for the Waterfront apartments my firm was building began cancelling the remainder of their staged payments. To be frank I would have done the same.

This meant the Waterfront development was little more than a valueless pile of concrete and worse still the post-dated checks I'd written to the Emirates flyers: the return of their investment plus a profit weren't worth the paper they were written on.

To make matters even more perilous an Iranian fraudster associated with another development absconded with a shed load of my company's money; but more about that 's.o.b,' in a later chapter.

Ultimately Abu Dhabi's ruler Sheikh Khalifa bin Zayed al-Nahyan saved Dubai from total economic collapse with a trillion U.S. dollar bail out, but Peter Margetts's Hampstead and Mayfair had no financial fairy godfather up the road.

The pilots had lost their life savings and me and my company had gone bust.

I'm not a quitter. I was ready to fight like crazy to refloat my sunken firm Hampstead and Mayfair and rescue something out of the wreckage for the pilots.

For starters I'd retained some of the pilots' U.S.$7 million: around U.S.$1 million was left in an escrow account and they could have that back.

There was however a trickier problem. The pilots were due a guaranteed thirty percent profit from apartment sales. That wasn't happening because there were no apartments to sell.

I had several meetings with the understandably incandescent pilots and offered to transfer what was left of the money they'd loaned me to another building project, but they were having none of it

At one stormy get-together one said: 'Come on, Peter, sell one of your planes or your yachts, and pay us back.'

'Planes? yachts?' I queried.

'You've got to be joking. You think I'm Donald Trump or something. I'm not in that league!

'I've gone bust too, fellas,' but for some reason they didn't believe me.

To add to my woes, it wasn't only furious pilots hammering at my office door and knocking at my home threatening to call the police unless I gave them their money back.

Another client, a colonel in the UAE Army, pitched up at the office, dressed in khaki camouflage fatigues, with four other officers.

'Pay me back, Margetts,' he threatened, 'Or, I'll take you to the desert, shoot you in the back of the head and bury you. No one will ever know.'

He scared my staff and I to me shitless when he pulled his pistol from its holster and placed it gently on my desk to indicate he wasn't kidding.

Believe me, he meant it. A UAE Army Colonel definitely could have got away with murder with impunity.

Trembling in a state of fear I frantically paged through our dwindling company accounts on my laptop and I did manage to scrape together about U.S.$100,000 to pay him off.

With all this turmoil in my life you will understand I was

already having trouble sleeping and had started drinking wine heavily, although I was relieved to find I wasn't the only property developer in desperate straits in the last months of 2008.

Dubai's real estate body RERA had called a crisis meeting. RERA, by the way, stands for the Real Estate Regulatory Agency, a body set up by the Ruler Sheikh Mohammed in 2007, which to this day proudly sports the optimistic slogan: 'Innovation, happiness, trust,' which always makes me smile.

A mass gathering of businessmen in the same predicament as myself was a comfort: we were like wildebeest herding together before crossing a crocodile infested river.

As I walked into the RERA building I and others were not optimistic RERA was going save us from the crocodiles' jaws because the Dubai quango had a poor reputation of making policy up as it went along to suit its own ends. RERA was also perceived as being totally skewed toward protecting investors rather the courageous and dynamic construction companies, which had risked so much to turn Dubai into a world class city-state.

As expected, the emergency RERA meeting was noisy and chaotic. Angry developers, like me, demanded to know if the Dubai Government had a rescue package in the works and vitally: was the Ruler going to suspend the bounced checks laws which to that would result in many of us being thrown in jail?

'No,' was the emphatic, although not entirely unexpected, reply to both questions.

'We're all fucked, absolutely fucked, and you just don't care,' screamed a furious Pakistani developer from the back of the hall as he pointed to red-faced government officials who shuffled their papers and eyed the exit doors.

Loud cries of agreement with the Pakistani man's allegation shook the hall to its rafters before officials swiftly made their excuses and left.

I drove home in despair and my general gloom worsened when I read an article by a partner at top draw accountancy firm KPMG.

He'd calculated if a property developer lost say U.S.$5million in a deal, then through a process known as building out on several other developments, he could recover the money.

That's the good news.

The bad news: building out would take an investment of another U.S.$25 million just to get the original U.S.$5 million back. I didn't have that amount of ready cash.

I was in a total daze. I could still reach out and embrace my precious wife, Susan, and my daughter, Olivia, but I felt physically sick at the thought of being separated from them if I was sent to jail.

My depression was so profound and it's even painful for me now, more than a decade later, to recall my sadness during the dying days of 2008, just before my arrest.

I finally knew the end had come when my corporate lawyer, Ludmilla Yamalova, called me for an appointment. We agreed to meet at Dubai's Ritz Hotel.

Californian Ludmilla was blonde, chic and still in her twenties when I first instructed her, and she's currently a prominent Dubai lawyer hosting a regular radio phone-in show.

Here's a interesting sidebar: Ludmilla hit the headlines in 2009 when she and a male companion were on vacation in Yemen and were kidnapped at gunpoint by tribesmen. They were freed after the U.S. Consulate in Dubai negotiated their release.

But back in 2008, Ludmilla was a relatively junior attorney working for a prominent, British registered law firm in Dubai: Mac Davidson.

She'd overseen all my property development contracts and in the plush surroundings of the Ritz that day I had serious questions to raise with her about due diligence on The Waterfront project.

But my immediate concern was: how to recover the pilots' money from escrow so I could make them a settlement offer and get them off my back?

Her reply stunned me: 'Well Peter, we can try through the courts.'

'The courts, Ludmilla? The fucking courts?'

I couldn't believe what she'd just said.

'But that could take years!'

Apparently, court action was the only way in these circumstances and there was more very bad news: 'My next question is: where do I stand legally on the security checks I wrote to the pilots? They're going to bounce.'

In cold, legal tones Ludmilla replied: 'If the security checks were written in bad faith, then the police will claim a criminal offence has been committed.'

'But I didn't write them in bad faith.'

'It doesn't matter, in Dubai there's something called strict liability on checks. Bad faith is assumed.'

'Jesus, will I go to jail then?'

'Yes, if one of the pilots goes to a bank and presents a check for payment'

'Peter, my guess is you'll be arrested, face trial and you'll get three years.'

Just as I was assimilating that bombshell she added quickly: 'In the light of that, I'm going to need another 100,000 *dirhams* (U.S.$30,000) for my services on account, and you'll need a criminal lawyer now, so that's further 100,000 *dirhams*.'

That night I went home utterly shattered not believing the disastrous chain of events that had befallen me and my family.

I found little Olivia, my daughter, asleep in her cot.

Gently, I picked her up in my arms and laid down on the bed. Then, I clutched my child tight across my chest, and wept.

To understand my story properly there's one more element to explain, so you get the full picture.

It wasn't bankruptcy *per se* that landed me behind bars. It was Dubai's draconian check laws.

Say you were an executive renting an apartment in Dubai on a year's lease. Your landlord would usually ask for a signed check for the first month's rent dated, let's say: January 1st.

But, at the same time, he'd also demand eleven additional signed security checks, post-dated for February 1st, March 1st, April 1st and so on.

In the great scheme of things, and if everything went to plan, the landlord would cash each check as the first of every month rolled by and everyone would be happy.

However, there was a huge Sword of Damocles in this check payment system prevalent in Dubai in 2008.

What happened if a fraudster cleared your bank account, or you got made redundant, or for whatever reason, there wasn't enough money in your account to honor the post-dated security check cashed later in the year, say: in August?

In Dubai the law was clear: if you signed a security check that your bank couldn't honor, you'd not only committed a civil offence, but also a crime, known by lawyers as an absolute offence, which carried automatic jail time.

Crazy, I know, to be prosecuted and sent to prison for something that wasn't your fault, however that's how things rolled.

I wasn't alone. In 2008, the year of the world economic meltdown, thousands upon thousands of Emiratis and expat Westerners and Asians had already signed millions of post-dated security checks, for apartments, mortgages, limos and sport club memberships.

Many of the companies they worked had gone bust meaning there were no salaries paid into dwindling bank accounts. The banks showed no sympathy, they simply didn't honor the checks.

The guys I felt sorry for were executives who'd signed security checks on a corporate account, in their roles as finance officers. They were still deemed criminally liable and faced prison.

With so many thousands of checks bouncing like rubber balls sheer panic swept through Dubai's white collar, expat, workforce.

Rather than face arrest expat parents yanked their kids out of school, packed up their homes, fired the maid, grabbed suitcases and hightailed it to the airport for a one-way flight home to the States, Europe or Asia.

Such was the speed of the exodus countless high-end limos and people carriers were found abandoned at the airport carpark coated in sand blown in from the desert. The petrified forest of sand-coated SUVs was a bizarre and poignant symbol of Dubai's economic collapse.

Susan and I could have done the same thing: closed our home, gathered up Olivia and our possessions and left Dubai forever. And you're probably wondering: why didn't we?

We talked about it for hours and in the end decided to stay put.

We both loved Dubai's lifestyle, and I felt very bad for the pilots. I wanted to reimburse them somehow.

This meant I had to pull something out of a hat and got down to work on the rescue package involving another 'off-plan' build, which, I mentioned earlier, they rejected.

At the same time, I'd written to them begging them not, under any circumstances, to try to cash the post-dated security checks I'd written to them from the original deal.

I explained with no money in my company's account the checks would bounce and I, as CEO, would be arrested and packed off to jail, then they'd get nothing.

One day in late January 2009 one of them decided to ignore my pleadings and presented his check at a bank for payment.

4

The early days

And, so, my first full day as an inmate in Dubai Central jail which, if you're interested, is twenty-five miles east of the city in a sand-blown furnace known as the Al Awir desert.

The 'big-house,' is one of the largest in the Gulf. Officially it accommodates around four thousand inmates, unofficially: thousands more.

I'd cleared quarantine and prison guards escorted me to Building B, cell block B1, a wing reserved for the so-called check cases, a catch-all term for Dubai's businessmen banged up in jail after the collapse of the city-state's economy.

Trying to get a feel for the place I asked guards about the lay of the land. They explained the female and juvenile sections were in a stand-alone building away from the main blocks and the hard cases: drug barons, paedophiles, murderers, rapists and other violent criminals were housed in Building A, next to Building B.

The guards told me I'd get a chance to meet them at recreation and meals. Something to look forward to!

Block B1 was long and narrow. Each floor had twelve cells which looked for all the world like shipping containers. Perhaps they had been once. And at the end of the corridor of cells I saw a sparse communal area with a television, a table and four public telephone boxes; but no other basic comforts, like chairs!

The guards just abandoned me in B1 with my bag of possessions. I must have looked lost, like a kid on his first day at school.

'You alright mate?' an inmate shouted jovially from down the corridor.

Maz Akbar was a plump, British Pakistani, in his forties dressed in white prison pyjamas two sizes too small for him.

'I guess so, I just arrived,' I smiled back.

'Checks?' he said

I nodded: 'Yes.'

'Me too, I've been here four years now,' he said rather nostalgically, like describing his time in a retirement home.

'Four years, Jesus,' I muttered to myself, having noted Maz's casual acceptance of such a long jail stretch for signing a dud security check.

'Hey! You there. Yes, you!' another English voice boomed down the corridor. I swiveled around.

'You a Brit?'

I nodded again.

'Right, get yourself in here with us mate. Make it sharpish, before they put you in another cell full of twats.'

Dave was a former British Royal Marine, about six feet six inches tall, built like a brick shithouse, packing biceps like Popeye's. He told me he came from a gentile town on England's South Coast.

Very much in the tone of an army drillmaster Dave barked: 'You take that top bunk, mate.'

It was then I learned new arrivals were always assigned the top bunk.

'The bog, the wash-sink and shower are through those swing doors,' he said, pointing a sinewy arm in the general direction.

'Oh...this guy here: he's Martin.'

The Martin in question was sitting on a lower bunk; a pale-skinned, fair-haired, German businessman, in his early forties. He was very urbane, well educated, and being German spoke with perfect English, of course!

He turned out to be another check case, like myself.

I introduced myself as Peter Margetts, I wanted to make that clear; I wasn't Peter Nicholas, as jail records and Dubai's law enforcement had me mistakenly listed and unpacking my meager bag of possessions: clothes and toiletries Susan had brought me, I gave my cellmates the short version of why I was in jail.

Then, as it was lunch time, we trooped off to the canteen and sat down.

Grinning as he spoke: 'Make the best of lunch, Peter. It'll be your main meal here. It's always, rice and... something,' said Dave.

'Monday, is rice and chicken, Tuesday: rice and fish; the fish is usually rank by the way, so make sure you fill your boots with rice.'

'Wednesday, is rice and roadkill.

'We call it roadkill because neither we nor the cooks know what meat it really is.

'Then it's rice and chicken for the other days.'

Dave added: 'But you don't have to eat that rice shit all the time, Peter.'

'You can order a sandwich, but you'll need to fill in paperwork to order...then it takes a week to deliver.

'Book your sandwich on Monday and it arrives the following Monday, simple as!' he laughed. So did the others.

I really appreciated Dave's dry humor and was already beginning to enjoy the British chumminess; the traditional stiff upper lip mentality; the ability to appreciate the funny side of being forced to wait for a week for a cheese sandwich.

And as I sat around the canteen table and looked and listened to Dave, Martin, Rob and other inmates, for the first time since my arrest two weeks before, I felt relaxed and most importantly: safe.

Yes, I was in jail, but I didn't feel alone. I was among down-to-earth, good men caught up in the same nightmare as me: decent guys who arguably shouldn't have been in jail at all, separated from loved ones; the so-called check cases, harshly punished for a crime unique to the Gulf region.

Glancing at the faces round the table I thought: 'God bless you lads for making me feel welcome.'

Looking back, I see I wrote in my diary:

'Compared to Al Rashidiya, the violent hellhole I just endured the last few weeks, Dubai Central is fucking paradise...the Ritz.'

On reflection the description Ritz was a bit strong, and, as you will hear, the feel-good factor wasn't to last very long.

After lunch I told former soldier Dave I was interested in football and boxing. As a sportsman himself he enthusiastically showed me around two exercise yards; one the size of a five-a-side football pitch, the other much bigger: a huge quadrangle with four legs supporting a massive canvas canopy like the ones you see at international expos, protection from Dubai's blistering summer heat and occasional winter rains

'We usually run around the track anti-clockwise, mate.'

'Running clockwise doesn't feel right, for some reason,' Dave remarked wistfully.

I was happy to take his word for it, although I didn't understand his reasoning at the time.

Back in our cell I got a chance to talk some more to Martin.

He was the CEO of a Hamburg-based luxury yacht building firm. He'd had a falling out over a business deal with an Emirati prince up the coast in Ras al Khaimah.

The prince knew there wasn't enough money in Martin's firm's account to honor a large post-dated security check that Martin had signed over to him. So, the prince presented the check to a bank for payment knowing it would bounce, which resulted in Martin being thrown in the slammer.

The yacht maker put on a brave face, but it was clear he was repressing rage behind his calm exterior; as he told me his story he gritted his teeth and subconsciously banged his knee with a clenched fist in frustration.

I felt an affinity with Martin. We'd both fallen in a ghastly black hole from which escape seemed impossible. Him sharing his story helped me come to terms with my dire situation.

As for Dave, I learned he'd held a high-powered post in Dubai with a top-end German carmaker and had been found guilty of fraud. He insisted he was innocent and was appealing against sentence. He was also at pains to reveal he was married to a glamorous East European lady. Dave told me little more on that front; I didn't push him, but I guessed there was an interesting backstory.

I should mention there was a fourth man in our cell; an unusually silent Indian; not even a cursory: 'how are you?'

passed his lips. I learned from the others he spent his days with fellow Indians on another wing and returned to our cell only to sleep.

And so, on my first night, I climbed up into my top bunk and settled down to sleep. It's at night you realize you're in jail, but I counted my blessings in a strange sort of way.

Yes, I was in a very bad situation and like the other check cases I felt deep anger and utter shame of being behind bars; had my mother been alive she would have been devastated.

Also, I was in a prison cell with three men I barely knew, instead of being at home in bed with my beautiful wife. And in the next building, a few feet away, were more than a thousand violent criminals.

But unlike Al Rashidya detention center, in Dubai Central my cellmates seemed like decent guys and no one meant me harm, apparently. That was a plus.

I said to myself: 'Don't worry, Peter. You're going to get out of here.'

'You can get through this. It's not so bad.'

Lying in darkness I listened intently to the sounds of prison: the distant crunch of locks being turned, the muffled Arabic conversations of guards coming on night duty, other inmates coughing or moaning in their sleep, the hiss of the 'air-con.'

Then my eyes closed.

Prison diary, January 24th 2009:

My friend, John, set up a Facebook page called 'Justice for Peter Margetts.' Some Emirates pilots had posted: 'Margetts is a crook.' The pilots also claimed I'd been stopped leaving at Dubai airport with £4 million pounds in a suitcase! What bollocks!

Prison diary, January 25th 2009:
Inmate Billy told me he's leaving jail soon. He had a vacant look in his eyes. I thought he was going over the edge.

My first day behind bars morphed into a week and I found myself falling into prison routine surprisingly quickly.

Getting the day started always seemed painfully slow. At each new dawn Dubai Central Jail struggled to its feet like a reluctant, fully laden camel, facing a tedious desert trek, spitting and scrambling to get on its haunches.

At 5 a.m., the '*Allahu-akbars*' of the Muslim call to prayer blared from scratchy speakers inside our cell and boomed out from bigger ones in the corridor, the signal that it was time to get up.

At 5.45 a.m. breakfast started, definitely not the so called full-English! Not even Continental, Dubai Central's 'brekky' was a single boiled-egg in its shell, a bread roll and a cup of tea or *chai* to wash it down.

'Looks like you'll be losing a few pounds in here,' I muttered to myself, tucking in for the first time.

My right knee was aching for some reason and late one morning I hobbled to make my first phone call to my wife Susan. With the time difference, she and our one-year-old daughter, Olivia, would be up eating breakfast.

I was dying to speak to Susan; our last contact was at Al Rashidiya detention center two weeks before, when both she and I had been in pieces.

At the time I begged her to get out of Dubai and take Olivia with her, especially as she'd received visits to our home by off-duty Emirates pilots demanding money. Susan had absolutely nothing to do with my business affairs, so the pilots' actions were totally out of order.

I'd already heard through phone contact with my brother-in-law Karsten, who lived in Dubai, that Susan had taken my advice and found a house to rent for herself and Olivia, in Richmond in West London.

I stepped into one of the telephone cabins to make the call to London. The booth was a tad old fashioned with wood framed windows like those in public buildings in England in the 1950s. But when the folding doors closed with thud I was in isolation, no inmates or guards to bother me, no prison loud-speakers, a sort of soundproofed telephone haven.

Other prisoners told me Dubai's intelligence service routinely listened to prisoners' calls, but I didn't care. I needed to speak to my wife, soak in the warmth in her voice, hear her saying she loved me, and if the spooks were tuned in: so what?

I'd bought a U.S.$7 phone card from the canteen; I tapped in the code on the card and my heart started to pound as I listened out for the familiar British ringtone across the squelch and static of a very bad line.

It was pure bliss to hear Susan pick up and her sweet: 'hello.'

My heart jumped. I wanted to tell her how much I needed her, how I loved her. And there was so much more to say; so many questions, but being British we kicked off our conversation about the weather!

According to Susan London was under a blanket of snow and for a second or two I visualized Richmond's roofs glistening white, reed banks on the River Thames shimmering with frost and bundled up commuters picking their way along icy footpaths to the Tube station. Such a world away from my own address.

Then, the important stuff: Susan said she and Olivia were OK and getting used to life in West London. She told me my business partner, Kieran, had shut my company down and laid off staff. That was fine by me and the right thing to do.

After some chat about Olivia's sleep routine and my brief snapshot of life behind bars I was hoping Susan would throw me an emotional lifeline and utter those magic words: 'I love you Peter.'

But they never came. Instead, after a minute or so, our conversation turned as frosty as London's weather.

My wife suddenly lashed out: 'Peter, you've been an absolute idiot, I've got no sympathy.'

And the 'ear-bashing' continued along the lines of how could I put her and Olivia through such a nightmare? The collapse of my company was: 'all your stupid fault,' she said.

At first, I couldn't believe what I was hearing. But Susan went on: 'I told you not to get involved in risky business deals, you're to blame for all this mess,' she sobbed down the line.

I hit back: 'Hold on a minute, aren't you supposed to be my supportive wife? My so-called rock?'

Silence, and yet more silence from the other end; there was nothing, apart from crackles on the line.

'I'm in fucking jail, Susan, and missing you and Olivia like hell,' I cried.

Still no response, just static.

Susan didn't need to say anymore, her silence said it all. I'd got the message.

At that point I was so stunned I had nothing further to say.

Suddenly an inmate started hammering on the phone box

door to be let in. I could see he wasn't going away, so I had to put the receiver down, still in shock from my wife's response.

I trudged back to my prison wing in a daze of despair.

Seeking solitude in my cell, hurt beyond words by what I'd just heard from Susan, I glanced around at Western and Asian inmates who'd obviously been in Dubai Central forever.

Most were expat check cases, like me, and I could see what years in jail had done to them: grey men with grey thoughts, their sad, unseeing eyes reflecting nothing but the bleakness of their prison surroundings.

But there was more. My fellow inmates were like zombies and I discovered later they'd taken a cocktail of over-the-counter drugs such as pain killers handed out by the jail's medical unit. That's how they spent their days under a drug induced semi-coma.

I asked myself: how could once respectable businessmen, energetic entrepreneurs and captains of industry, with loving families waiting for them at home, have turned into lost souls, drugged to the eyeballs, slumped in chairs like sacks of rubbish?

Tears welled in me for a few seconds as I realised that I could end up like them if I didn't get out of that place.

Then, as if an unseen hypnotist had clicked his fingers, my inner strength kicked in again, as it had in Al Rashidiya when I'd hit a low.

'Hold it together, Margetts. Come on man, you will survive, and you will get out of there.' I told myself.

My usual antidote to a stressful day was to slip on trainers and go for a serious run; I mean ten kilometres at least.

I looked out of the window on our wing. A curtain of clouds drew across the sky above the jail; it might even rain, I thought, but who cared if I got wet?

I hopped it to the exercise yard and started bashing out a few hundred laps, alone, pounding the track in a clockwise direction.

But then, I recalled what cellmate Dave told me on my first day in jail.

And, you know, he was right.

For some cosmically profound reason running anti-clockwise at Dubai Central felt so much better.

*Prison diary, January 30th 2009.
A couple of prisoners tell me, they are praying for me, which was very humbling.

*Prison diary, April 9th 2009.
I've a feeling my wife, Susan, and daughter, Olivia, are slipping away from me. That's really killing me to the deepest part of my body and soul.

Before I tell you about a big decline in jail conditions and the start of my downward spiral toward a very dark period in my life, I must mention a bright ray of light on an otherwise stormy horizon.

As the weeks slid by, I was enjoying more cordial phone chats with my wife, who had, as you'll recall, initially blamed me for the calamitous events that had left me behind bars.

I cherished the fact our relationship had much improved because she was my link to normal family life outside prison. And our young daughter, Olivia, of course, was a massive part of that.

Susan and Olivia had moved from London to another European capital to be closer to Susan's family. She asked me not to disclose exactly where in this book, and I respect her wishes.

Our once-a-week phone conversations opened a window on wonderful world, way beyond the barbed wire and walls of Dubai Central and the most banal detail meant the world to me.

Such as: she'd taken Olivia to the park that morning, Olivia had been thrilled by her first tram ride; all enchanting minutiae that sparked images in my head, not only of my wife and daughter enjoying life, but also of the park's lushness, of fussing ducks on the lake and sleek, silver trams.

Those phone calls were a true mind trip, only someone behind bars in far-off, sweltering, Dubai could really appreciate, and I will always be grateful to Susan for that.

Better still, as Susan chatted away telling me about her week, in the background I heard little Olivia babbling to herself as toddlers do, or the clatter of her toys on the wooden floor.

What really lifted my heart was when Olivia knew I was on the line talking to Susan and she shouted: 'Daddy!' It was a wonderful reminder to me, despite my absence, I was still part of her life.

One day she yelled: 'Daddy, Daddy, when will I see you, when are you coming home?' which made me cry.

But I don't want to sugar-coat the phone relationship too much. From those same conversations with Susan I began to have doubts about our marriage lasting and that raised worries about being able to stay close to my beloved daughter which, was so important to me.

Olivia had been just over one-year-old when I was arrested and what tore me up was that I might still be stuck in jail when I should have been helping her to write her first words, or playing hide and seek, or seeing her off on her first day at school, like any ordinary dad.

'Peter, I'll make sure you always have a relationship with Olivia,' was a cryptic line Susan dropped into one conversation, from which I understood our marriage might be in trouble, but my access to Olivia was going to be OK.

When I wasn't on the phone, I daydreamed about the two of them during my waking hours. I dreamt about them most nights. One recurring scenario was of Susan and Olivia dressed in white gowns both running toward me with open arms.

Sounds cheesy, I know, but those glorious, fantasy images helped me get through another day behind bars. It also helped with the loneliness I was starting to feel.

But, phone calls and daydreams about my family didn't always work. On odd days I was completely overcome by the sadness of separation and I cried, but I made sure I didn't weep in front of my cellmates whom I respected. They all had their own problems without me blubbing!

There were other psychological pressures. Caged with thousands of other prisoners you may be surprised to hear me say I became lonely.

Whilst it's true myself, and cellmates Martin, Dave and the others spent long periods chatting together, we slept in bunks feet from each other, we ate together, exercised together and oftentimes laughed together; but like most prisoners anywhere in the world, at day's end we were on a very private journey of our own.

And in our claustrophobic, thirty-two-square feet world our closeness went only so far, up to an almost palpable barrier in terms of mental and physical connection which none of us crossed or wanted to cross.

On top of that, as months slipped by, I'd made a private pledge to keep myself to myself: 'Be polite to prison guards, be cordial with other inmates, stay fit, keep your head down and do your time Peter, however long that turned out to be.'

That was my personal unspoken mantra and although a feeling of loneliness might have been the downside, it was a philosophy that served me well in the troubled times ahead.

Prison diary, April 29th 2009.

Settled into a daily routine: 5-45 am, breakfast, weekdays, cornflakes. Friday and Saturday, eggs, yippee! 7.30 am, 200 -400 sit-ups. 7.45am, 5 kilometre run. Work out with an African guy who used to box. 10.30 am, shower. 11. 15 am, or 12.15 pm, lunch, depending on first or second sitting. 1pm: crossword. 2.30 pm: football. 4.30 pm, shower 4.45pm, dinner, often not eaten. 7.30pm, read/watch TV, 10.30 pm, sleep.

When I first entered Dubai Central I hadn't been fully aware of the jail hierarchy, but I quickly learned about the much-feared dons: organised crime bosses, with years of violent criminality under their belts, who arguably had more power than the prison governor.

Here I'm talking about the hardest of men among hundreds of villains jailed for first-degree murder, armed robbery, assault and rape of both women and men in a country where a life sentence meant life.

It was hard to avoid meeting the dons and their henchmen during two-hour exercise time: the toughest being from Russia, Ukraine, Georgia, or from Asia including drug barons from Uzbekistan and Afghanistan.

I also rubbed shoulders with Emirati mobsters from the, little publicized, Dubai underworld. They were based in neighbourhoods, like Al-Warqaa and Al-Quoz.

You recognised a don easily. Most strutted about the place like dictators; muscles like boulders, with thick, sinewy necks. Some, I noted, had no discernible neck at all; you couldn't tell where their head ended, and their body began.

All dons ran protection and extortion rackets to which prison bosses turned a blind eye. How did they work?

Well, most prisoners had access to a small amount of cash, say a hundred dollars a month. Other prison currencies included telephone cards we could buy in the canteen for the equivalent of U.S.$7, or cigarettes.

Protection from a beating could be bought with, say, a handful of phone cards and a bit of cash.

And if you didn't play ball: there was very big chance you'd come to serious harm because the dons and their fawning acolytes, who were usually loud-mouthed pipsqueaks several inches shorter than their bosses, usually packed homemade weapons made from aluminium canteen plates sliced into quarters with edges honed razor-sharp, or they'd unscrew hinges from toilet doors which they ground to make fearsome blades; or any weapon that would gouge or cut.

The threat of rape was also a potent persuader. The dons controlled a handful of Arab prisoners who were blackmailed or paid to screw an inmate until he handed over his phone cards, cigarettes or cash. Just the threat of being taken up the arse in the toilets, without a condom and gel, was usually enough to make anyone hand over cash without argument.

As I mentioned before, I'm pretty fit and wiry. Whether it was my physical shape, or just my deliberate, low profile demeanor, I never felt pressure to pay for protection in Dubai Central.

That wasn't the case at Al Rashidiya, where I was held first. That wretched place was a violent jungle where hair-trigger crazies were always spoiling for a fight, for no reason other than they didn't like the look of you.

There was one guy: a rough looking *bedoun,* a stateless Arab, with long untidy hair, who'd had been staring at me since I'd arrived; I could see from his hate-filled eyes he wanted to do me harm, presumably just for the hell of it, because I'd done nothing to him.

'You need to find yourself some protection, Peter,' I said to myself.

Perhaps my guardian angel was watching. There happened to be a lump of a man in his forties, with an easygoing manner, stretched out on a mattress close to mine.

He was Moosa, from Cameroon, six feet three inches, 280 pounds, a former heavyweight boxer and in happier times a Dubai nightclub bouncer.

Moosa had good English, the smile of a Cheshire Cat, dazzling white teeth and the kind of easy manner most Africans I'd met in Dubai usually had.

I discovered we both shared a passion for football, in particular, we were fans of Albert Roger 'Mooh' Miller a Cameroonian footballing legend who grabbed world headlines for his on-the-pitch twerking dance after scoring a goal.

Older readers may remember it was Milla who powered his side to a two-three advantage over England in the 1990 World Cup.

I also learned Moosa was a boxing fan, and I quickly sensed the muscled Cameroonian was probably good man to have alongside in a tight spot.

After a gossip about football and boxing it seemed an appropriate moment to mention the *bedoun* who'd been spoiling for a fight.

Moosa smiled: 'Don't worry, Peter, I'll look after you. You are my brother!'

That evening, as prisoners settled down for the night, a bunch of drugged young Arabs, I'd dubbed them the 'ratpack', began picking fights, as a way to pass the evening.

As they headed in my direction Moosa suddenly sprang to his feet like a leopard preparing for a kill; veins visibly throbbed in his neck, muscled arms outstretched, fists like hammers.

'If any of you try anything, I'll tear the first one apart with my bare hands,' he yelled.

The 'ratpack' stopped in their tracks.

'Then I'll kill the rest of you, one by one.'

For a few moments the world stopped turning in violent Al Rashidiya; the sudden silence sucking all the life out of the chamber.

Who would blink first? The 'ratpack' weighed up the odds of surviving a fight with the Cameroonian colossus.

He knew, and even in their drugged-up state, the ratpack knew the answer, and eventually one fluttered his eyes signaling submission and mumbled: 'OK *habibi*.' 'No problem, *mafi mushkela,*'

Then, they slunk off to harass some other poor bastard.

The *bedoun*, like every other inmate, had watched the tense stand-off. He never tried to stare me out again.

Thank you, Moosa, wherever you are now.

Although I did my best, it was very difficult to avoid the jail's bad guys, the misfits, society rejects.

At the beginning of my sentence they were housed in the next block. But because of overcrowding, or when they'd caused trouble on one wing, they'd be transferred to ours.

Salim was an Emirati nut-job serving a long stretch for raping a boy. He was in his thirties, bearded, a bit on the chubby side, probably with Sudanese ancestry.

After he arrived on our wing he was always itching for a fight. To deliberately antagonise the lads, he'd stand in front of the TV so nobody could see the screen, just waiting for one of us to ask him to shift his fat bottom. If we told him to get out of the way, he got belligerent.

One evening he picked a fight with one of my favorite inmates; indeed, we all had affection for an elderly Indian guy we nicknamed Hawk-Eye.

Like me, 75-year-old Hawk-Eye was a businessman and another check case. He was serving fifteen years, which for him was effectively a life sentence.

Hawk-Eye suffered severe diabetes and groaned in pain if he had to stand or sit too long.

Medics took pity and had allocated him a grubby plastic chair to sit on to watch TV. This was a great privilege because the rest of us had to flop down on the floor. There were no chairs.

One evening, thuggish Salim snatched poor old Hawk-Eye's chair away from him claiming it was his. He then started bashing and kicking the Indian, forty years his senior.

At first, to our amazement and admiration, Hawk-Eye fought with distinction and landed a few blows.

But it was always going to be an unequal battle and Salim rained punch after punch on the poor old-timer until he collapsed and passed out on the floor.

I was on the point of wading in to rescue Hawk-Eye when another English lad grabbed my arm saying: 'Peter it's not your fight, leave it.'

In a split second, I realised he was right. Salim had brutish associates and retribution against me would have been swift and painful.

I renewed my vow not to break my golden rule: keep a low profile.

From April 2009 onwards conditions in jail ran rapidly downhill putting a massive mental strain on prisoners and jail staff. There was one main reason: overcrowding.

On the outside, Dubai's stringent bounced checks laws were being vigorously enforced, often without mercy.

One British businessman had a stroke and was fighting for his life connected to an oxygen tank in a Dubai hospital. The cops didn't care, and he was told if he survived he faced three years behind bars after corporate checks he signed had bounced.

Those Westerners who could flee Dubai did so, but thousands of businessmen like me, who'd decided to stay, found themselves arrested, tried and shipped to Central Jail on an industrial scale.

Soon our wing became packed to capacity with sixty men confined to ten cells most of the day and night.

Overcrowding also meant, in terms of accommodation, the old dividing line between white-collar criminals and hardcore killers, drug dealers and rapists, became blurred.

I started making a list of new inmates on our wing. My diary entry read: '*Cell 1: Ali (Rape) Abdullah (armed robbery) Fouzi (bounced checks) Ibrahim (bounced checks) Cell 2: all Pakistanis, one convicted murderer serving fifteen years, rest of them bounced checks and credit card debt. Cell 3: Mohammed Youssif property developer: serving nine years. Youssef Ali: serving nineteen years, Dirn: serving three years Harry: serving three years,*' and so on.

To add to our general discomfort exercise hours were also cut, so we were also locked up for longer with perhaps only an hour out of our cells each day.

The intense confinement of men at such close quarters for so long lead to tensions, especially as we had only bunks to sit and sleep on and the only entertainment, apart from banter among ourselves, was a TV and a ping pong table.

Put simply, we became very stressed and petty incidents that previously would have been laughed off before overcrowding, like a prisoner snoring or a turd not flushed down the bog, led to bad-tempered squabbles between inmates.

Throughout these early months I'd kept my sanity by staying in regular phone contact with Susan, although even then I could never predict what her mood was going to be; generally, it was good or cordial at least.

I also stayed out of trouble, hoping my good behavior could win me a reduction in my sentence, which, for all I knew, was between one and three years. I wasn't sure exactly.

I figured if I was a model prisoner, they might let me out after one year.

Hell, I was naive, but at the time, I didn't know what was around the corner.

5

Life sentence

Prison diary, June 22nd 2009, Friday -the Muslim holy-day -is soul destroying because the normal snail's pace of jail life shudders to a complete halt. I've been able to do 200 sit ups to try to stay fit.

Prison diary, June 26th 2009, I'm beginning to realise this jail's a place of heartache and stress and for me making light of it with dry English humor is the best way to cope. But I found humor doesn't always translate even among native English speakers.

It was summer 2009. And although months in prison had a mind-numbing monotony to them: call to prayer-eat-shower-shit-exercise-eat again-sleep-call to prayer; you could never exactly predict what the day would bring.

Out of the blue one of the guards casually announced British Embassy officials would be stopping by, news which sparked a bit of a buzz on our wing; some inmates were more impressed than others.

I actually punched the air: 'The cavalry are on the way, they'll get me released,' I exclaimed.

I skipped off to the exercise yard: 'I'll be free soon, thank God!' I shouted, to nobody-in-particular.

And sure enough, mid-morning a dozen or so British inmates, including me, were corralled together and then ushered into a special interview room for the meeting.

We were mostly check cases, but the gathering of cons included one or two bad guys from the secure unit.

The party of three from the Embassy were led by British Vice-Consul Mandy Smith and she'd brought with her: a Syrian-born lady who worked for the British and a man: a Foreign Office mandarin from London. I didn't catch their names.

They were all in their forties, seemed friendly and eager to help.

I was immediately drawn to Mandy. She had swept-back auburn hair, grey in places, and a kind, slightly pale face. She wore a tight-fitting, navy, trouser suit. With her full lips and Irish charm, she was certainly a sight for sore eyes in our all male world.

Yes, OK, I confess, I did fancy her a bit, mainly because of her striking looks and a soft Irish accent, which reminded me of Linda, an ex-girlfriend.

Getting down to business and preparing to make copious notes, Mandy asked us to speak out loud, in front of the others, about why we'd been imprisoned and how we thought the British Embassy could help.

First up: a bombastic British guy called Jim, the most wired and vocal in the room. He'd been tried and convicted of murdering his girlfriend and faced a possible execution by firing squad. He strongly denied killing the young woman and had a court appeal pending.

He said the grounds of his appeal were based on the Dubai cops not being able to find a body.

Jim claimed under UAE law he couldn't be convicted of murder if there was no corpse, which in its simplistic way kind of made sense, I thought.

Mandy and the other two officials listened attentively. But, I wondered if, like me, they'd been struck by Jim's bland narration of his story and his apparent lack of anguish his girlfriend was even missing, let alone dead.

Next to speak was Peter, a former British Marine serving ten years for drug smuggling. I'll always remember Peter. He was originally from somewhere in the Cotswolds, in the west of England, and a kinder more thoughtful man you couldn't meet. How he'd got mixed up in drug smuggling baffled me.

Peter was diabetic and said he needed urgent help from the Embassy because he wasn't getting his regular insulin supplies, without which he could slip into a coma.

'If I don't get my insulin and the right amounts of it, I'm going to die in here,' he pleaded.

Mandy promised she'd investigate.

Then it was my turn. I looked at Mandy for a moment and thought of phrases to convey my sense of despair and frustration at being behind bars for an offense which to that I felt was not my fault.

I didn't want to get too overwrought; after all Mandy wasn't to blame for me behind bars, so as calmly as I could I told her my story and that I needed the British Embassy to get me out of jail: *pronto*.

You see, prior to that meeting I'd been under the impression when Brits were in trouble abroad the local British Embassy would kick bottoms, pull out all the stops, organise legal teams, hell, even get a minister to ask questions in Parliament if necessary, where there'd been an obvious injustice, like the check cases.

How misguided I'd been. Mandy offered little comfort. She said the British government was aware how many of its citizens were languishing in jail because of the collapse of the Dubai economy, but: 'We can't, in any circumstances, interfere with another country's legal system. It's not possible for the British government to do that,' she said.

She added in a bland tone: 'What we're limited to doing is looking into complaints of ill-treatment, alerting the prison authorities to any medical conditions and providing you with a list of lawyers or interpreters.'

In other words: naff all, I thought; my words, not hers. Then, having run through what was clearly standard patter, Mandy softened a little,

'The Embassy can help with your criminal case, but only to ensure proper legal procedure is followed. First, you need to find lawyer. I can give you lists of attorneys. When you've picked one, he needs to contact us in writing.'

'This is important: your lawyer has to be an Emirati national to appear in the criminal courts,' she added.

I thought of saying that I did have an Emirati lawyer, Omar. He stiffed me for thirty-grand, never to be seen again! But I held my tongue.

As the Embassy team packed away their laptops and files and said their goodbyes, I sensed Mandy was someone who might go above and beyond foreign office guidelines, in other words she'd help me if she could.

That lifted my spirits a little, as my thoughts turned to finding a new lawyer.

*Prison diary, July 5th 2009.

An Australian couple, former clients, have filed fraud charges against me thinking I had money! They're mad.

*Prison diary, July 10th 2009: I met an inmate, an astrologer, who told me things are going to get better for me and predicted I'd released December 18th this year! The guru said I was too aggressive, and I needed a gold ring with topaz mount on my second index finger to calm me!

I realised I needed to act on Mandy's advice and engage an Emirati criminal lawyer, even though my sense was they were complete incompetents and rip-off merchants.

Nevertheless, I chatted to another inmate who recommended someone called Abdullah, who, by chance, was former head of the Dubai police department investigating financial crimes, including check cases.

Perfect man for the job, I thought. Abdullah was due to visit the jail the following week and I managed to wangle an appointment.

Abdullah was in his sixties, a tall and distinguished looking silver fox who could have passed, on a dark night, for the late Egyptian Hollywood star Omar Sharif.

Apart from his matinee idol looks I couldn't help but notice an ultra-expensive Mont Blanc pen glinting in the top pocket of his white *dishdasha*. I wondered: 'Perhaps he's going to surprise me and write something down, or maybe he only stirred his tea with his pen?'

As he relaxed in his chair, I also noted his black, brogue shoes peeping from beneath his *dishdasha*, so highly polished they shone like diamonds.

'OK, tell me your story, my friend,' he said.

In common with all Emirati lawyers, Abdullah carried no papers, files or even a brief case, and as I ran though my case, as expected, he left his pen in his pocket and just listened.

Minutes of my narrative went by and at first Abdullah nodded along, listened attentively and absorbed the story. Then he seemed to lose concentration. I'd seen that before.

It's a curious thing: the ancients of Arabia were super-intelligent. They invented the wheel, the written word, and Koranic lithography, which is simply, stunning. They perfected early surgery and gave the world algebra. It was hard to square all those incredible achievements with some of the modern-day Arabs I met in Dubai, many of whom seemed to have the attention span of a gnat.

Meeting over, non-committal Omar Sharif was hard to read. Thankfully he agreed to take me on as a client and ended our conversation with a simple: 'Let me see what I can do, Mr. Peter.'

His words weren't exactly the gung-ho, let's go get 'em' assurance I was hoping for, but as he stood up and we shook hands I found his air of quiet confidence reassuring.

I slept better that night than I'd done for weeks, but then, I didn't know life was about to take a horrid twist.

Prison diary, July 17th 2009: British guys Dillon and Abbas say they will be 'leaving soon.' I realise many inmates often tell you the same story: 'I'm going next week,' but they never do. Sweet Jesus, what a nightmare.

Prison diary, July 27th 2009: Some of the best lads in here are Africans. They have nothing and I can see they're treated like shit, but their spirits are normally bright. God bless them!

The most catastrophic day in my life began with the amusing 'ding-ding-dong' chime of Dubai Central's public address system.

UK readers will know exactly what I mean when I say the sound reminded us Brits of the TV comedy series Hi-de-Hi!

In that show actress Ruth Madoc's holiday camp announcements were heralded with her tapping out 'ding-ding-dong' on a kid's xylophone into the microphone.

Dubai Central's Tannoy was much the same in terms of a chime. However, the chime was not followed by: 'Good morning, campers!'

Instead, all we heard was a guard's strangulated tones calling out names of prisoners due for court that day. He sounded like he was stumbling through the pages of an international phone directory and with the same level of interest.

Suddenly my ears pricked up. Among the mangled names like Mohammed, Salim and Tariq, I managed to decipher, 'Peeeeter Neekolas, Peeeeter Neekolas.'

Who was this Peter Nicholas? I fumed. I'd been in prison seven months and they still hadn't got my name right. Nicholas was my middle name, not my surname.

But that wasn't my biggest immediate concern. My real worry was I was being packed off to court for a hearing and there was no way I'd be able to get hold of Abdullah my lawyer at short notice. I'd be on my own for what I understood was going to be an important hearing.

I thought: better be in court without an attorney than miss it. So, I lined up to be handcuffed with around seventy others, mostly Europeans, Asians and one or two Emiratis. Most of us were check case guys.

The big, blue school bus swept out of Dubai Central jail onto a busy freeway where the Asian driver slammed his foot down hard.

I hadn't found a seat and trying to stand up in handcuffs was tricky as the bus swayed drunkenly in and out of lines of traffic.

When we eventually came to a halt at a major traffic light snarl-up, I peered out of the bus windows and observed them: businessmen and women; the morning commute; fingers tapped at steering wheels; car radios were tuned to a Dubai music station or a CD played.

In happier times most of us businessmen on the prison bus would also have been behind the wheel of a limo driving to the office, or being chauffeured there, and sat in the same traffic jam.

So, were the commuters a little curious about the men on the bus in prison pyjamas? Did they wonder who we were and why we were in handcuffs? Did they realize, but for the grace of God, it could have been one of them on the bus and not me, if they'd fallen foul of Dubai's cruel check laws?

Probably not; most stared at the road ahead quietly fuming they'd been caught in traffic or they gossiped into their hands-free to families and friends. It all seemed so normal, another world to mine.

A half-hour later we pulled up at Dubai's, main criminal court, the Court of Misdemeanors.

My first visit to that bastion of legal ineptitude had been a couple of days after my arrest at a hearing which I described in an earlier chapter as: The Mad Hatter's Tea Party.

On that memorable day my former lawyer Omar made a brief, cameo appearance, had a falling-out with the judge, never returned any of my phone calls and was never seen again. Meanwhile, I'd been packed off to jail.

Enjoyed your thirty grand fee, Omar?

Since then I'd had dozens of quick, up and down court appearances lasting no more than five minutes and I was getting used to the chaotic routine of almost daily jail-court-jail trips.

As usual I was shoved into a heaving mass of several hundred other prisoners in an underground dungeon.

As I waited for my case to be called, I was overjoyed to spot another check case Brit: Kev Draper; a terrific, down to earth character who, before his arrest, ran a Dubai company that turned over five million bucks a year.

Kev and I passed the time rabbiting on about what we'd do when we were released from jail; a popular and perennial topic.

Then, there was a sudden, distant commotion. At first, we ignored it.

That was until an agitated guard rushed toward us yelling: 'You British...British men, come, come, *yellah! yellah!*

Both Kev and I were hurriedly bundled down a corridor beneath the courts where the guards flung open a cell door.

Inside was a raging bull: a man, foaming at the mouth and screaming a panoply of obscenities in English. Indeed, he was English. It was our friend, Peter K., the man who'd complained to the British Embassy's Mandy Smith about not getting his insulin supply.

'He's British, you're British,' yelled one guard. 'Get in there, jump on him.'

'Go on, get in, hold him down,' cried another guard.

Both Kev and I hesitated because Peter, poor guy, was going absolutely, berserk, and we could have got hurt tackling him.

But the impatient guards didn't wait and roughly shoved Kev and I in the cell with Peter, who was clearly extremely disturbed and violent; then they slammed the door shut.

I half turned looking for a way out and noticed the guards peering through a cell window clearly enjoying the entertainment value of me and Kev about to subdue someone who'd lost his mind. They were like Romans enjoying a fight at The Colosseum.

I looked at Kev and he looked at me. It was do or die, so we both dived on Peter who was immensely strong and flayed like wounded beast.

Somehow, we managed to find the strength to get a grip of his limbs and held him down. Then, one of the cell's doors opened and two nervous male Filipino nurses appeared. One brandished a hypodermic needle. A straitjacket would have been more use.

He plunged the needle deep in Peter's arm. It had no effect. Peter still struggled and screamed, poor man.

The nurse reloaded. And pow! Another tranquilizing shot into Peter's arm, that time a dose big enough to fell a horse. It worked; Peter stopped kicking and swearing, slipped into unconsciousness and was stretchered away.

The drama over Kev and myself were left panting from exhaustion, although luckily, we were both unscathed; not so much as a scratch.

Then, as if nothing had happened, the guards reappeared and bundled me upstairs to court to face a judge who seemed bemused, then slightly irritated, why I, the prisoner in the dock, was so red-faced, sweating and disheveled.

'Peter Neekolas, step forward,' shouted the court translator, I use the description translator in a loose sense.

'Sorry, I'm so sorry to be a nuisance, but before we begin: my name is Peter Margetts, not Peter Nicholas,' I corrected him.

'My surname is Margetts. I'm Peter Margetts.'

'Peter Neekolas, did you sign this check?' asked the translator, speaking on behalf of the prosecutor.

At the same time, he held the check above his head and waved it to the court. I could see it was one of forty-two I'd written to the pilots as part of the failed Waterfront property deal.

'Yes,' I nodded, as I'd done dozens of times before in previous hearings when asked about other identical checks.

The judge then jabbered something to the court clerk in Arabic, banged his gavel on the desk and signaled to the guards to remove me from court back down to the holding cages below.

It was all over in around twenty seconds, like my first court appearance months ago, and all the others in between.

As they led me out of court I protested loudly to the guards and to anyone else who'd listen that my lawyer hadn't been with me in court, I neither spoke nor understood Arabic, in short: what had just happened was a fucking farce!

On the bus back to jail I silently raged at Dubai, its rotten legal system, its joke judges and lawyers and at the hopelessness of my situation, trapped in the same nightmare as other Brits like Kev and Peter K. the man we restrained at court.

Once through the gates my mood wasn't improved by a robust pat-down from prison guards and being sniffed by dogs used to search out drugs; they weren't domesticated canines, but snarling devil-dogs specially bred for Dubai's security services: a cross between a jackal and a husky.

Returning to my cell I can honestly say I was at my lowest ebb in the whole wretched story thus far; unaware that awful day still had another sting in its tail.

Later that evening I was chatting to a guard I'd struck up a loose friendship with.

Mohammed was totally familiar with the injustices surrounding check cases and was sympathetic, as indeed were most prison staff, including the governor.

I told him about my court appearance earlier and how a court official had produced a single check and had asked me if I'd signed it. I said I wondered why they kept doing that on each court visit.

'Mr. Peter, each time you go to court they'll show you a check and ask if you signed it, said Mohammed.

'You're right, ' I said: 'they're doing that for every check I wrote to the pilots.'

'Mr. Peter, you should know you're being sentenced to a year in jail for each check.'

'But I signed forty-two checks,' I murmured.

'Well, that means forty-two years in jail for you,' said Mohammed, as if we'd been discussing a fortnight on the Costa Brava.

I was so taken aback by what I'd just heard, I couldn't speak for a moment.

'Forty-two years? At my age, that's a life sentence.'

Mohammed had no reason to fret. It wasn't him.
'I suppose you're right, Mr. Peter, sorry for that'

6

Escape plans

*_Prison diary, Christmas Day 2009: Guards allow British prisoners to hold Christmas lunch in a room set aside for us. We tucked into Pot Noodle with Heinz tomato sauce, spaghetti and Xmas cake made from Swiss rolls. Thirteen of us in total. We joked it was the 'Last Supper.' Prisoner Mark sketched a picture of us._

*_Prison diary, January 2nd 2010: Lawyer tells me I'm serving the longest prison term of any foreign national in jail in the United Arab Emirates. Never been number one before!_

How do you get your head around a forty-two year prison sentence? I kept saying the number over to myself as I struggled to process that thought in my brain. I'd be eighty-six when I got out, that's if I lived that long.

I'd prepared myself for up to three years in Dubai Central; I could manage that if I needed to. But forty-two years? No fucking way.

I'd contacted a pal, British barrister Richard Gray, who'd raised my case with my British Member of Parliament at the time, Susan Kramer. She was told by the Dubai authorities my release date would be 2041, if I behaved myself and remained a model prisoner.

What I couldn't get out of my brain was: months before I'd been working my socks off as a respected businessman, I'd taken care of my family, made money for myself and my clients and created hundreds of jobs in the construction industry.

Now, I was in jail, effectively facing a life sentence for no other reason than that Dubai's economy had crashed and burned, condemning me and thousands of other expats into purgatory behind bars.

You could understand why I was struggling mentally and why, at times, I sought solace and emotional support from other inmates in the same dire straits as myself.

One of them was Jonny Jouty, a middle-aged, intelligent businessman with dual Indian/Canadian citizenship and a warm heart.

He'd been jailed for three years for writing one bounced check for U.S.$40,000 and, like me, he was desperately missing his family.

I think we spoke almost every day about freedom and how getting out of jail was going to be a new beginning for us and our families.

He told me he dreamt of the moment they opened the prison gates to let him go, but meanwhile he fretted about his wife and kids having to cope without him around as head of the family. Indians have very strong sense of family loyalties, so I felt deeply for him.

'I worry about them all the time, Peter. I don't know how they're getting by without me. I must get out of this place,' he confided.

I know Jonny drew strength from me as much as I found

support in him and he got me through some very dark days of depression.

One morning I bumped into Jonny walking in the opposite direction as I headed to the exercise yard.

His normally cheerful eyes looked sunken, his sallow complexion had a grey tinge. He didn't look at all well.

'Hi Peter, I don't feel so good. I'm going to the main office to report sick and try to see a medic,' said Jonny.

'OK good luck, I'm sure you'll be fine,' I said

I thought nothing more of our conversation. I enjoyed my morning run and eventually jogged back to my wing, where an inmate pulled me to one side: 'Have you heard?

'Heard what'

'Jonny's dead.'

'Massive heart failure.'

Poor Jonny left a wife and two children aged four and eight and there's absolutely no doubt in my mind his heart attack was brought on by the stress he suffered from being in jail. It's anxiety that gets all of us in the end.

And, I was a hundred percent certain he'd have been alive today, had it not been for Dubai's rotten check laws that put him in prison.

I not only mourned Jonny's passing, which was another huge psychological blow for me, but I also came to a shocking conclusion.

That could have been me, I thought to myself. Death might come to me sooner than freedom.

For a moment I thought, maybe Jonny's been lucky; he was out of it and at peace.

*Prison diary, January 12th 2010: Cellmate Martin is serving eighteen years and his wife at home is struggling to cope. He's spoken about killing himself. She's studying to be a lawyer to help get him out of jail.

*Prison diary, April 27th 2010: I can't think of anything rationally. I'm too upset -too pissed off with life. A few months ago, I was a respected property developer living with my wife and young daughter in Dubai. Now I'm in a hellhole with druggies, murderers and thieves battling a corrupt and utterly inefficient, joke legal system, with no chance of freedom for me.

Although I held the unwanted honor of the having the longest sentence of all British prisoners in the UAE, my jail term paled alongside Emirati tycoon Abed Al-Boom.

A judge had clobbered him with 923 years and nine months!

Think about it: a millennium behind bars in Dubai Central!

Forty-two-year-old Al-Boom was a legendary Emirati wheeler-dealer who'd earned a fortune in property development. One factoid is crucial to this story: he was a close friend of the Ruler Sheikh Mohammed and very much part of the royal circle.

Al-Boom had it all: forty-three fast cars, numerous luxury yachts, private jets and glamour models flocked to his infamous parties.

He was also famed for his generosity, handing out top-of-the-range motor cars to local footballers and other celebrities.

'You played brilliantly Mohammed, have a Bentley my son!'

Socialite Al-Boom was among Dubai's serious A-listers but his glittering, glamorous world came crashing down after he was accused of swindling a third of a billion dollars from investors.

Prosecutors alleged wily Al-Boom set up bogus investment schemes for 4000 clients and from time to time doled out small payments to the poor fools to con them into thinking the schemes were genuine and generating a return.

Local media gave the story of Al-Boom's prosecution massive coverage and a buzz ran around the jail when we heard about his almost 1000-year sentence.

As fawning guards led him with over-the-top courtesy through our wing local Emirati prisoners either threw themselves at his feet or kissed his hand. It was unbelievable.

He was a short man, boyish looks with thick lips, bushy eyebrows, a dark complexion and a bit on the chubby side with grey stubble, in real life not exactly the jet-set magnate I imagined him to be, but he seemed pleasant enough.

And after the rock-star welcome and applause finally subsided Mr. Al-Boom was duly installed in the cell next to ours.

New prisoners were normally given a top bunk or forced to sleep on the floor. Not Al-Boom; guards kicked another inmate from a cherished bottom bunk and invited the new arrival to take it.

'For you, *Sayed*,' the guards cooed.

I don't know why we were so surprised, but Dubai Central's newest inmate wasted no time in finding himself a butler! He was an Indian inmate called Firaz, an ever-jovial guy in his sixties who enjoyed dying his hair various dark colors using cigarette ash dissolved in water. He readily set about butler duties for a small fee.

Firaz's main duties were to bring Al-Boom's meals for him in his cell, or wherever he'd parked his carcass, and to massage his master's feet on demand!

But for all his bravado and the idolization he enjoyed from Arab inmates the tycoon's first night in jail was surely a massive fall from grace for a man used to sleeping in five-star hotels and palaces.

That evening when the hurly-burly and razzmatazz of his arrival had died; when lights were being switched off and doors locked by guards; I heard a sobbing sound from the cell next door, which grew louder to a wail.

I went to investigate. It was Al-Boom, tears streamed down his puffy cheeks: 'My, God, how am I going to get out of here?' he cried.

I thought of saying, 'that's what we all wonder, matey', but decided not to upset him even more.

As I revealed Al-Boom had friends in very high places and after a week or so, none other than Dubai Ruler Sheikh Mohammed intervened to save his bacon.

He ordered the shamed businessman be set free on condition he paid a third of a billion dollars into a special account, for distribution to investors, many of whom had lost their life savings.

Somehow Al-Boom found the money, set up a treasure chest and began the payments process.

The Ruler did something else. He also ordered no civil or criminal proceedings could be brought against Al-Boom if investors were reimbursed, effectively letting the alleged fraudster off the hook.

To their credit Dubai prosecutors tried again to nail Al-Boom on further charges, but it was never going to fly after the Ruler's decree.

So only weeks after Al-Boom had been sentenced to a

millennium behind bars I and the other lads returned from exercise one morning to find he'd gone.

The fabulously wealthy jailbird had flown, without so much as a: 'see you down the golf club fellas!'

Talk about one rule for one and not for the other.

I yearned to be released from jail so I could set up a financial rescue plan to pay the pilots back. They wouldn't let me.

But then my name was Peter Margetts, not Abed Al-Boom!

Prison diary, April 28t 2010: Lt. Colonel Mohammed Thani Al Fashi, Dubai Central Jail administrator speaking to a local newspaper: 'Not everyone in jail is a criminal, there are a lot in here who are good and great people. I hope they're able to get back in the community soon and live their life.'

Prison diary, April 30th 2010: Very angry at what's happening to me. Ran fifty laps around the exercise yard in forty-degree heat and didn't even break sweat. I did 500 sit-ups and the same number of push-ups. The legal system here stinks.

What is it about prison escapes that captures our imaginations and inspires Hollywood script writers?

We marvelled at actor, Steve McQueen's heroics in *The Great Escape*. Fictional Andy Dufresne wowed us in the 1994 movie *Shawshank Redemption*; desperate guys in prison boiler suits unscrewing ventilation grills, scrambling though air-conditioning pipes, drilling through steel bars to crawl to freedom; ahh... the glamour of it!

As many of us caged in Dubai Central were serving long stretches, it'll be no surprise to you that we inmates openly discussed escaping over the big wall in search of liberty.

I can't say escaping was a daily conversation topic. We idly mulled over our various options perhaps once a week, especially when I or one of the lads spotted a prison door that shouldn't have been left ajar or a slapdash repair job on the twenty-one feet high, perimeter wall.

Getting over the wall wasn't the only escape route. We agreed court appearances were another chance to dash for freedom as the prison bus normally parked three feet or so from doors to the underground holding cells, leaving a gap.

I met one young Iranian inmate who arranged for a buddy to be waiting on a Mitsubishi motorbike, engine running, close to where the bus pulled in.

He stepped off the bus, hopped nimbly through the open gap between the bus doors and court doors and onto the back of his pal's bike. The pair disappeared in a cloud of exhaust fumes and screeching tyres.

But the Iranian's freedom was short lived. Dubai cops rounded up his entire extended family of nineteen, including children, and made it clear they wouldn't be freed until he gave himself up.

And that was the point. Once you made it over the wall, or did a runner from court, how did you escape from Dubai itself, especially Western men with no passports?

It was common gossip in jail there were corrupt officials at Dubai Airport who, for U.S.$50,000, could get someone without a passport on an Emirates flight to pretty much anywhere. Boarding other airlines like British Airways or Qantas was no-go. It had to be Emirates. None of us set much store by that story.

But, if the airport wasn't a realistic option, that left only sea or land routes for a getaway.

People smuggling out of Dubai Creek was, and still is, a thriving and lucrative sideline for corrupt boat skippers.

Fees were negotiable but for around U.S.$30,000, or perhaps a gold ingot, Iranian, Indian or Pakistani *dhow* captains would hide an undocumented stowaway below decks, no questions asked.

But how useful could they be to Western males like me? The *dhows* were heading to their home ports, so even if I had a spare thirty grand and I found a bent skipper I didn't want to be dumped on an Iranian beach with no passport. The mullahs would likely have ordered me thrown in jail for being a British spy!

What's more, I didn't like the sound of being dropped off on a moonlit night in Karachi or Mumbai docks with no papers. The Indians or Pakistanis would certainly deport me back to Dubai. And even if I made it to the British High Commissions in New Delhi or Islamabad there was no guarantee they wouldn't send me back to Dubai.

So, a plan to escape by sea, also looked like a no-no for a white, Western male.

How about by land?

Saudi Arabia was out. The border was very tight, and the Kingdom was effectively a dead end for a Westerner with no passport.

Oman perhaps?

Definitely, no. Not after I'd heard this story about a fellow Briton; let's call him Jim.

Businessman Jim heard what had happened to me and feared

he was about to be arrested for bounced checks.

Rather than face the same fate, he opted to leave Dubai on a land escape route through Oman and agreed to pay U.S.$50,000 in cash to people smugglers. That was: U.S.$25,000 upfront and the rest paid at the end of the journey.

The smugglers were Emiratis, and their plan was to disguise Jim as an Arab 'bedouin.' The fact he was a blue-eyed, fair-skinned, blondish, middle-aged Brit hadn't fazed them.

For the first stage of his Lawrence of Arabia transformation the gang ordered him to stop shaving for a week and to buy some brown-tinted contact lenses. So far: easy enough.

And at nightfall on the evening of the escape they kitted Jim out in a grubby *dishdasha* and they used a flannel to rub a cup of cold coffee into his face. His own mother wouldn't have recognised him!

Then they bundled Jim into a Jeep-type vehicle and headed to the Al-Harjar mountains, a border region between the UAE and Oman.

Frontier guards at the UAE checkpoint nodded the motley crew straight through with the *bedouin* asleep in the back, no questions asked. So did the Omanis, who didn't even bother to ask for papers.

Once across the border in Oman, Jim was expecting to head under his own steam to Muscat and to work on an escape from there by air or sea. Not a bit of it! The Emirati smugglers handed Jim over to Omani gangsters at gunpoint. They told him they were driving at least two days south to the border with Yemen.

Lawless Yemen had definitely not been part of Jim's Plan A, however he had no choice but to go along with it; not wanting to be shot and robbed of the U.S.$25,000 stuffed in his backpack.

Getting across the frontier from Oman into Yemen wasn't a sophisticated operation.

With terrified Jim cowering in the back seat, the driver revved the Jeep's engines to 'full-whack,' let the brakes off and ploughed through massive sand dunes that marked the border, like an express train smashing through snowdrifts.

The noise of a van hurtling at speed through mountains of sand, engine roaring, alerted sleepy-eyed Yemeni and Omani guards who lit up the fleeing vehicle with their truck headlights.

Then, they opened up with machine-gun fire.

Astonishingly the Jeep, with Jim in it, crash-bang-walloped safely into Yemen under a hail of bullets; none of the occupants suffered so much as a scratch, including lucky Jim.

From the border it was a two-day ride to the capital Sana'a.

But Jim didn't have a passport to buy a ticket. And here, you must admire his chutzpah.

He told British Embassy officials a cock-and-bull story that he was a round-the-world yachtsman and he'd lost his passport overboard during bad weather, off Aden.

To his amazement the Embassy bought it and issued Jim a new British passport. Next day he was on a flight to London.

That's a great tale of derring-do, but as desperate as I was to get out of Dubai, making a break for it by land, sea or air seemed like a risk too far for me: a family man with a young daughter who needed me in her life.

Prison diary, May 1st 2010: The prison phones weren't working. I prayed someone, somewhere on the outside was trying to get me out.

Prison diary, May 3rd 2010: Got a bad feeling about rising tensions on our wing.

On the subject of escape plans, Dubai's Ruler, Sheikh Mohammed, had set up an astonishing challenge for every prisoner.

At the end of 2008 he'd declared Central Jail so secure he threw down the gauntlet and offered U.S.$1million to any prisoner who managed to escape!

Silly man.

A million bucks was a lot of money, especially if you were a couple of dirt-poor, migrant workers, like a pair of prisoners I spotted looking a bit shifty and out of place in the exercise yard one day.

I learned, one was Ali an Iranian; the other Qais from Afghanistan, and both were in prison for burglary.

I couldn't but notice the pair, in their twenties, were as thin as rakes, which was unusual because there was always food around the jail, either in the canteen or among inmates.

I also noticed their prison pyjamas were all-white, which was slightly odd as their shirt tops should have carried a colored stripe to denote the length of sentence they were serving.

But, dress code wasn't always enforced, and I knew it was possible to buy an all-white strip, so I shrugged off suspicions the pair were bogus, even though something wasn't quite right.

From time to time Ali dropped into our wing to scrounge coffee from other Iranian inmates. In recent days that had become more regular.

Some inmates remarked on the amount of coffee Ali was getting through but in the great scheme of things, with other important issues to occupy our thoughts in Dubai Central, we told him to take as much coffee as he wanted and wished him well.

Then, a few days after my encounter with Ali and Qais in the exercise yard, all hell broke loose.

Sirens at the prison sounded and the entire jail population was lined up in corridors for a 'head-count.'

That's when we heard Ali and Qais had done what Sheikh Mohammed foolishly dared to suggest was impossible: they'd escaped!

The jailhouse really buzzed. We inmates were full of admiration.

'They've cracked it! Wow! Fuck yeah,' we yelled and high-fived each other.

The big question was: how the hell they'd done it?

The rumor mill worked overtime and the consensus was this: first, the pair had unscrewed a ventilation hatch above a phone kiosk on an upper floor of their wing and scrambled inside it.

I examined a similar hatch. The opening was incredibly narrow, barely enough to squeeze a human body through. That explained why Ali and Qais were so thin. They'd been on a crash diet ahead of their escape.

Then, from the ventilation shaft they'd dropped down into an open yard and ran undetected to the outer seven metre high wall.

The main wall was unscalable without a rope ladder, which they didn't have. That didn't matter.

Workmen had carried out renovation in recent days and had replaced a stretch of concrete wall with a temporary metal door.

Like moles Ali and Qais had burrowed through soft sand under the makeshift door to reach desert scrubland beyond and freedom.

As prison search parties set off, we heard the crafty pair escaped detection in the desert because they were wearing sand colored, pyjamas, which acted as camouflage.

So that's what they did with our coffee. They'd used it to dye their all-white pyjamas.

Nice touch boys!

No doubt with hearts pounding and adrenalin surging the pair of 'Houdinis' successfully crossed a stretch of desert and eventually reached Dubai city thirty miles away.

But here's the kicker. Wait for this!

From downtown they telephoned prison governor Lt. Colonel Al-Hakim and asked how they could claim the Sheikh's one million dollars!

How fucking cheeky was that?

I regret to say there was no million-dollar reward and no happy ending for daring Ali and his Afghan pal.

In Dubai the pair of fugitives had gone their separate ways and Qais was found by a security guard hidden and asleep in a false ceiling in a city apartment block. He was handed over to police, given a beating and hauled back to jail in short order.

Meanwhile, cops caught up with Ali partying in an upmarket hotel nightclub!

Both escapees were thrown into solitary, a concrete-clad hole in the ground where prisoners were held in chains with no bed and in virtual darkness for weeks. How any man could survive solitary, none of us understood.

There's a postscript to this fascinating escape story.

Weeks later I spotted a guard giving prisoner on the ground a good kicking; the back of the victim's shirt was stained with fresh blood.

As I walked closer, I realised the prisoner taking the thumping was Iranian Ali whose skeletal and wasted body had shrunk to around a hundred pounds after his time in solitary. He was so horrifically thin and so despairing in appearance he reminded me somewhat of a German concentration camp victim.

'You poor sod,' I murmured to myself.

It turned out guards were taking him to the Iranian Embassy in Dubai because the ambassador had asked about his welfare!

What happened next to Ali? You'll have to wait for later chapter, because we'd not heard the last of him.

Prison diary, Friday June 11th 2010: World Cup starts and a testing week ahead. I must keep myself in check before I absolutely lose control, simple events like another inmate not flushing a turd in the bog have become massive issues!

Prison diary, June 27th 2010: Week started badly: I get fifteen of my appeals rejected and sentences were up all upheld. England get thrashed by Germany four-one and we're out of the World Cup, can nothing go right?

After Ali and Qais's escape there was a massive security crackdown. Prison head counts came thick and fast; day or night; whenever jail commanders felt like it.

Lights in our cells were left on twenty-four hours a day making it hard to sleep. My diary read: '*Lights blazing day and night. What a fucking nightmare*'

Doors normally left open were kept locked, including the main one on our wing, which was usually open to allow access to the canteen or exercise yard.

This and other tightened security measures not only made life miserable for us, it also pissed the guards off because they were forever opening and locking doors normally left ajar, so the jail could actually function.

Incredibly, despite the crackdown, there were two further escapes giving us inmates something more to cheer about and giving a big finger the Ruler's claim the jail was totally secure.

One night, a guard returned to block D in Building 1 to find cell doors open and inmates missing. How many escaped, or how many were caught we never found out.

But an Emirati prisoner aged thirty-two and a twenty-nine-year-old Iranian appeared in court weeks later.

The judge heard both were tech-wizards and had stolen a computer from the prison's main control room and removed two gizmos used for opening and closing cell doors. Somehow, they'd adapted the devices to open doors in Building 1.

Both were acquitted of theft because they accused each other and the judge couldn't make his mind up who, stole the gizmos! Yet another example of Dubai's fine justice system in action.

That wasn't the end of the jail breaks. Sheikh Mohammed's bold claim about Dubai Central being escape-proof took another embarrassing knock.

Three lifers in the drugs block: an Iranian, a Sri Lankan and an Afghan, and another Afghan serving a ten-year stretch, had the ingenious idea of positioning a set of football goal posts up against the outer perimeter wall during afternoon exercise time.

The goal's crossbar was already eight feet above the ground

and somehow, they used the netting and height advantage to swing themselves up and over the wall!

One broke his leg on landing and was arrested before he got very far, another escapee was picked up a couple of miles away. But two others were never seen again!

Incidentally, the Ruler Sheikh Mohammed never did honor his pledge to pay a million dollars!

Wait a moment, your Royal Highness. Wasn't I in jail for not honoring a check?

7

Sex, drugs... no rock'n roll

Prison diary, September 28th 2010: Martin was teaching me to sail and I was learning the different knots: how to tie a bow line / reef knot. It was navigation tonight, I laughed, there I was sitting in the desert learning to sail!

Prison diary October 18th 2010: Given notice I've got three court appearances, in three different courts on the same day. One of pilots' cases in court twenty, another bounced check case in five, another in court four. How can I be in three courts at the same time?

As I revealed earlier, the chances of getting caught after an escape were very high. Also, I couldn't face having extra years being added to my long sentence, as well as a stint in solitary as punishment.

So, there was no choice really. I had to survive mentally and physically, taking things a day at a time until some legal genius sprang me free.

The Gulf's steaming heat tested everyone's endurance and the ultra-hot months from June through the end of October was a sweltering, physical challenge for prisoners and guards alike.

July and August were the cruelest months. From around

seven-thirty in the morning temperatures soared to reach a furnace-like high of around fifty centigrade at midday. Some lunchtimes it felt like the gates of hell had been left open.

It was a heavy, humid heat that struck like a hammer blow the moment you stepped into the exercise yard. Crack an egg on an exposed piece of metal and it fried. Kick a football and it burst in the heat.

Within a minute of being outside prison pyjamas turned into damp rags, so generally it paid to wait until late afternoon to do any physical exercise.

Being able to exercise and run off some frustration was so important for thousands of men banged up in prison, many of whom were in their twenties and thirties with normal, but unsatisfied, desires.

It was rumored they put bromide in our water supply to curb natural urges, but I never believed that story.

Thankfully, there was only one guy on our wing who masturbated openly. Wolfgang, a large German, had absolutely no shame and barely covered his penis with a sheet as he stretched on his bunk wanking away without a care whilst other inmates walked in and out of the cell, including me. Looking the other way was all we could do.

Sure, we told him told him to pack it in. But he just ignored us. He didn't care. He was having a wank and as far as he was concerned, we could all fuck off!

I'm a straight man with no interest in the gay scene, but man-to-man stuff certainly flourished in Dubai Central. I'd heard through conversations with other inmates that the prison's Arab population had an interesting attitude to same-sex encounters.

Without getting too graphic, indulging in a bit of buggery after lights out didn't mean you were gay. Oh no! Not so long as you were the giver and not the receiver.

So, there were several Arab guys in our block who openly messed around with young Asian lads who, for cigarettes, a phone card, or a small amount of cash, would bend over and take one for the team.

When I was in quarantine, on my first day in jail, I was offered a long-haired, teenage Filipino by one of the guards. I declined. Later I overheard the two of them banging away in a cell close to mine after dark.

Then, if you were interested, there was another more exotic distraction, the prison's ladyboys.

To be frank, in the grim monotony of prison life, in a jail full of hairy-arsed men, the sudden appearance of a very attractive 'woman,' and some were stunning, believe me, was a joy to behold. In fact, one or two were so freaking hot, it was impossible to believe they were born male.

From time to time you'd see them sashaying along Dubai Central's bleak corridors like girls in Times Square, all dolled up in a mini skirt, ruby-red lipstick, mascara and perhaps a smudge of rouge. They were often a lot of fun.

One Friday morning, I was working my fitness routine of sit-ups and push-ups when I became aware someone was watching. I could smell a soft, sweet, fragrance.

As I looked up to see who it was, I heard a shrill, feminine voice sing out, 'Oh, I love to love, but my baby just loves to dance...'

In front of me was a beautiful Filipino ladyboy with luscious lips and long, dark hair. She twerked her butt and swirled like a lap dancer.

It was meant to be a big come-on, but I knew nothing was going to happen and so did 'she.' Such a laugh though; it really brightened up my day.

By chance, one of my pals had been watching: a prisoner called Kevin, a middle-aged, former London city trader who resembled Homer Simpson, we all thought. Kevin instantly got all loved-up. In my diary I wrote, '*He was all over her like a rat up a drainpipe. Sorry Kevin*'!

Over the next few days the pair sat on Kevin's bunk, cooing like a couple of lovebirds. But the closest they came to anything approaching hanky-panky was her massaging his toes for hours whilst serenading him with a sultry love song. I'm certain it went no further.

Although that's a vaguely humorous story; the ladyboys I met in jail were forever cheerful, but the reality of Dubai ladyboy life was far from happy. Tragic would be a better description.

Those in jail were mostly Filipino or Thai and, on the outside they'd worked in brothels, or as go-go dancers. They weren't in prison for prostitution, because Dubai turned a blind eye to the billion-dollar sex industry.

They'd been locked up for fighting with clients, petty theft from customers, or some other crime not at all connected to selling their bodies.

Of course, being thrown in jail hadn't been on their minds when they'd flown to Dubai from cities like Manila or Bangkok, often on fake passports bought on the black market.

Why Dubai? One draw was they'd heard the city-state had a more liberal attitude to sex. The bigger attraction was the mind-boggling money they could earn.

'The men in Dubai love me,' purred a Thai ladyboy to an, investigative newspaper reporter who was Asian.

'When I walk in the street Dubai or in the shopping malls, Arab boys are all over me.'

'Sometimes I earned a thousand dollars if I spent the whole night.'

She went on: 'I don't know why. Religiously speaking, it's forbidden. But culturally, that's different.'

Another, a Filipina, described why she'd left her village and family to pitch up in Dubai: 'The amount of money you can make is times ten, if you're able to maintain just one regular client.'

'If you have a working relationship with a guy, you can practically become a millionaire.'

But life for ladyboys was dangerous, deadly even.

Being beaten up or taken around a corner and raped in a dark alley at night was all part of the scene and a couple of years before I arrived in Dubai a ladyboy called Sally Camatoy, who featured in an art house documentary Paper Dolls, was found bludgeoned to death. Her killer was never caught

Even those who were arrested and faced deportation were at risk from violence and sexual assault when they were in custody.

Abuses of all kinds were reported, according to organizations that were promoting human rights. They included, beatings, public floggings and sexual violence, often at the hands of police or other security officers.

'They raped me. Some things are almost too bad to remember,' one ladyboy said, tearfully. 'The head of the police took me into a back room with other ladyboys,' she sobbed. 'That's where it happened. In the police station. We were forced to get naked, and they took pictures. There was terrible verbal abuse. I think that was worse than the rape thing.'

Another, named Mya, spent three months in Dubai Central when I was there.

After her release she told an Asian journalist about her horrific experience: 'The guards would throw hot water on me from outside of the cell,' she said. 'They would spit on me. It was awful and degrading. They didn't even look at me as a human being. They call us *haram,* which is something really bad or forbidden. That's what they call animals that they think are dirty. They saw me like I was a pig or a snake.'

Mya claimed guards used to put rope in her cell to torment her.

'They expected me to just hang myself,' she said.

'Nobody would care. But I told myself I never would. My life is too beautiful and too exciting to die in a jail cell.'

Mya also described how other inmates were allowed, to get to her in solitary.

'There were a lot of big criminals in there, drug dealers, things like that.

'Those big criminals were allowed to pay, to come to my cell.'

'The guard would open the gate and let them enter my cell and rape me whenever they wanted.'

'The harder I fought, the tougher it was for me.' she said.

She went on: 'The first month was the hardest. I fought like crazy. But after the second month, I realised I couldn't do it anymore, so I tried to be nice and cooperative.'

Mya ended her story: 'In the end, they just let me go,' she said.

'When they decided I had suffered enough, they released me, just like that.

'No court, no nothing.'

Prison diary, October 20th 2010: I called the British Embassy to ask where my law books were? And to mention my knee problem. I'd been waiting six months to see the doctor. Vice-Consul Mandy Smith said: 'be patient.'

Prison diary, October 28th 2010: Bit of good news. I rang home and Susan and Olivia were both on good form. I chatted to Olivia and she told me her mum was taking her for another tram ride. I was thrilled.

As I made clear in previous chapters, violence was part of daily life in Dubai Central, especially as overcrowding grew worse.

But inmates tended not to fight or cause trouble if they were zonked on drugs and, whilst never encouraging pill-popping, prison bosses definitely turned a blind eye to it.

Getting your hands on heavy hitters like opium, heroin, other hard drugs such as cocaine and the so-called zombie drug Spice was never a problem because, as I mentioned earlier, the jail's dons included some of the world's notorious drugs barons linked to the poppy fields of Afghanistan.

Stashes of hard drugs were mainly smuggled in by corrupt cleaners in the pay of underworld gangs or surreptitiously handed to prisoners during a visit to court.

One cleaning contractor was caught red-handed after he'd soaked a bundle of fifty-*dirham* notes in a crystal meth solution. They were found in a routine pat-down, meanwhile police in

Dubai City were often reported in the media as seizing ecstasy consignments destined for the jail.

A fix cost a modest amount of telephone cards, cash or cigarettes; equivalent to U.S.$10. But if you had enough prison currency the world was your pharmacy in Dubai Central.

I must make clear: heroin and other hard drugs were never integral to the lives of lads on our wing, that's not to say they didn't dabble in chemicals; far from it.

As I mentioned earlier in this book: they got their fix legitimately from the medical wing which readily dished out drugs which, on their own, were not hallucinatory, like Imodium for diarrhea, pain killers such as Ibuprofen, or just plain Asprin.

But, gulp down perhaps seven of those innocuous drugs at the same time, and boom! Happy dreams!

Prison bosses knew of their addictions. Of course, they did. But they didn't give a toss that check case inmates turned into junkies. Whilst prisoners were doped and happy, they usually gave no trouble and guards had an easier time of it, so it was win-win.

Drugs and ladyboys weren't the only forms of escapism in Dubai Central

Other inmates chose illicit hooch instead, but you needed a very strong constitution to drink Chateau Dubai Central.

Prisoners brewed it in the canteen usually from dates. If there were no dates, other fruit was fine. The yeast element needed for fermentation came from slices of bread.

Its color was ghastly puce, it burned your throat like hot coals, but my God, when it kicked in, it made our wing sparkle like Xanadu!

8

Shot at dawn

Prison diary, April 29th 2011: Watched royal wedding of William and Kate on TV. I was close to tears as I saw England looking its best. I realised I needed to get back home to the UK. I want to live the rest of my days there.

Prison diary, May 13th 2011: I concluded, in jail you're the only one who can lift your own spirits and stop yourself going crazy.

During my time in Dubai Central the jail housed twenty-four inmates on death row, mostly murderers.

All had automatic appeals pending and if they were turned down by the appeal court it was up to the Ruler of Dubai, Sheikh Mohammed, to sign a final execution order; until then, the condemned men languished in solitary cells waiting for Sheikh Mo's thumbs-up or thumbs-down.

It had been a few years since there'd been an execution in Dubai.

A Yemeni man found guilty of kidnap and murder was put to death in 2002 and there'd been eight more death sentences carried out elsewhere in the UAE, but none in Dubai until thirty-year-old Emirati boat skipper Rashid Al-Rashidi was led out to face a firing squad.

It had been 440 days since Al-Rashidi's heinous crime had stunned the emirate.

In November 2009, he'd lured a four-year-old Pakistani boy, Moosa Mukhtiar Ahmed, into a mosque toilet where he'd raped and strangled him.

Al-Rashidi had committed his vile crimes during the Muslim religious festival of *Eid Al Adha*, which is dedicated to sacrifice, making the shock even greater for the people of Dubai

Murder squad detectives arrested the boat skipper the next day based on fingerprint evidence found at the scene and he was quickly brought to trial.

During one of the early hearings I happened to be at court the same day.

As usual I was hanging around with hundreds of other prisoners in an underground holding area when there was a sudden commotion and screaming police sirens.

One prisoner shouted: 'It's Al-Rashidi!'

A diminutive man in his thirties with shoulder-length black hair, balding at the front, was bundled through the crowd close to where I stood, flanked by black-suited, heavily armed, riot police.

For a moment I reflected: why do most killers look like someone you'd bump into in the supermarket and wouldn't give a second glance to?

Al Rashidi looked straight ahead, with a terrified expression, as he was frog-marched though the crowd of prisoners up the stairs to court.

The chief prosecutor pulled no punches. He ran through a graphic description of the evidence and then jabbed a finger at the accused man in the dock and cried: 'You murdered an innocent angel in the house of God.'

Strong stuff, but, absolutely accurate.

The first court appointed attorney was so disgusted with the offenses he refused to represent Al-Rashidi and handed the case back to Judge Eisa Al Sharif.

The same judge appointed new lawyers, but they had no stomach to act as defence attorneys.

Finally, Al-Rashidi's case was picked by up one of Dubai's leading legal eagles: Mohammed Al-Saadi.

Once the trial got underway psychiatrists testified Al-Rashidi was a paedophile with an obsession for boys; crucially doctors insisted he was sane and understood the evil of his crimes.

In mitigation, Al-Saadi outlined Al-Rashidi's horrendous childhood and early life.

The court heard the killer's mother died giving birth to him in Bahrain. When he was two years old his father took him to the UAE, where the father settled and married an Indian woman who already had a couple of boys and three girls.

Al-Saadi said his client had been treated as an outcast by his new family and was blamed for anything that went wrong in the household. He wasn't allowed to play with his half-brothers and sisters and was abused physically and mentally by his stepmother.

'My client sniffed glue, smoked and drank alcohol from a young age, possibly as young as ten.' Al-Saadi told the judge.

The sad backstory went on: Al-Rashidi's father died when he was fourteen, that's when he dropped out of school and joined the UAE Army, only to be dishonorably discharged three years later.

A life of petty crime followed until he became a boatman working out of Dubai Creek.

According to defence attorney Al-Saadi, despite having a regular job the accused still suffered severe mental issues which had turned him into a 'savage criminal.'

But even Al-Saadi had to admit: 'This defendant, my client, is an embarrassment to humanity.'

The compelling evidence, which almost certainly sealed Al-Rashidi's fate, came from a police inspector who'd interviewed him and testified the accused had been: 'smiling and indifferent,' when confessing to killing the boy Moosa Ahmed.

After that evidence it was game over for the defence and on January 29th 2010, only two months after the crime was committed, Al-Rashidi was found guilty of rape and murder in Dubai's Criminal Court of First Instance. He was sentenced to death.

Prison diary, May 20th 2011: Friction rising on the wing between Johnny and Ali who nearly came to blows over something stupid. Two others were head-to-head: Azin and the Snouzer. None of them had learned in jail you need to bite your tongue, blend in, keep a low profile..

Prison diary, June 14th 2011: Tonight, cellmate Martin made a salad using fruit and garlic. I can't stand apples and oranges in salads, but I don't say anything. It's small treats which break up the mind-numbing monotony.

Al Rashidi was brought to Dubai Central and thrown into solitary. And, although he'd had a number of death threats from other prisoners, nobody managed to get to him.

The condemned man was left to rot on his own in a cell for fourteen months until all the appeals for clemency were heard and the Ruler, Sheikh Mohammed finally gave an execution order.

Not surprisingly a ripple of tension went around the jail when we learned there'd been no last-minute stay of execution and Al-Rashidi was to be shot the next day. None of us knew where, or the exact time.

On the Wednesday night before the day of execution, the condemned man's two brothers visited him for a final time to hug and say their goodbyes. He had no other visitors.

The guards told me on his last night Al-Rashidi had no appetite and had picked at his last meal of chicken and rice. He'd slept fitfully, finally waking a few hours before dawn to face his executioners.

'He was fasting when he died, and only drank a glass of water before the *Fajr* prayer call at around three thirty a.m,' said one guard.

The rest of the story I picked up from guards who'd witnessed Al-Rashidi's final journey.

They said the condemned man had showered and spent the rest of the time in prayer before being dressed in a black jumpsuit. He was hooded with hands tied behind his back, then put in a prison van and driven to an execution spot not very far from the jail; a bit of scrubland where Dubai's security services often carried out target practice.

Weeks before, the murdered boy's father, Mukhtiar Ahmed Khudabaksh, had repeatedly begged Dubai authorities to be allowed to witness the execution. The request had always been turned down.

However, at the last minute, police sent a car on the morning of the execution to collect the murdered boy's father, his mother Jamala Imdad and two uncles.

The condemned man was taken to the place of execution within sight of the jail. Guards said Al-Rashidi was pale and clearly terrified, but he stayed on his feet as he took his final steps. He asked to kneel in prayer one last time. Then, he was tied to a stake in front of a nine-man firing squad.

Only one of the shooters had a loaded rifle, the others fired blanks, a method designed to prevent them knowing who made the fatal shot.

Moosa's family huddled close by with the mother Jamala muttering prayers as the shooters took aim.

Dr. Ahmed al Haddad, Dubai's Grand Mufti, asked Al-Rashidi if he had anything to say.

'I want God to forgive me for what I have done,' he mumbled.

'I also want to tell the Moosa's family, I'm sorry.'

But the apology fell on deaf ears with the family.

'I will never forgive him,' Mr Ahmed told the Mufti.

As the firing squad raised their rifles the charges of rape and murder were read out and the sentence of death

In the moments before a fatal volley rang out Al-Rashidi's last words were,

'I witness that there is no God but Allah, and Mohammed is his messenger.'

From my cell, I and other inmates heard the distinct crack of gunfire at eight thirty-seven that morning; the whole wing fell silent for a short while.

At the execution spot Al-Rashidi's body slumped to the

ground and, Moosa's father was allowed to step forward, with a doctor to witness his son's killer was actually dead.

'Now my heart is at ease,' he whispered.

9

Double sadness

Prison diary, December 13th 2011: Bing-bong from the Tannoy. I was called for court. Dirk the German was in the prison bus with me. He's an accountant, not coping well with jail. I tried to cheer him up.

Prison diary, December 20th 2011: Mehul has been released. I'll miss. him. He left me all his things. Funny you built up a relationship with someone. They get released, never to be seen again.

Late November 2011 and I suffered a double whammy of sad news.

Guards entered my good friend Peter K's cell and found him dead in the toilet.

You'll recall Peter was a diabetic who complained bitterly to British Embassy officials he was having problems getting his insulin and warned he might die if he didn't get access to a more regular supply.

And I told you how myself and another inmate, Kevin, had to wrestle the poor fellow to the ground when he went mad at court one day, arms and legs flaying and foaming at the mouth. He was eventually sedated by two male nurses. Even after that harrowing incident he continued to complain about not getting insulin regularly.

Peter had an interesting backstory which to that I didn't mention earlier.

He was a former British Marine and had been arrested at Dubai's Terminal Three in February 2010 with a kilo of cocaine in ninety pouches in his stomach, which he'd swallowed. Customs officers also found almost another kilo taped inside his underwear and to his groin area; total street value in Europe was about U.S.$500,000.

Peter had flown in to Dubai on an Emirates flight from Sao Paulo, Brazil, and was planning to catch a connecting flight to Cape Town, South Africa.

He might have passed through customs undetected had the terminal's body scanners not broken down, meaning transfer passengers were subject to a pat down.

As Peter waited in line his shiftiness alerted officials that he might have something to hide. I'm not surprised he was sweating with half-a-million bucks of cocaine in his stomach and strapped to his balls!

After his arrest Peter pleaded not guilty at Dubai's Criminal Court of First Instance. To the surprise of no one he was found guilty of possession and smuggling a week later by Judge El Saeed Mohammed Bargouth, who hammered him with a stiff ten-year sentence and packed him off to join us at Dubai Central.

I'd known him over a year, and he'd become a good pal.

A few days after Peter's death the British Embassy issued a statement saying:

'A post-mortem is taking place and we have informed the

next of kin,' namely his wife and daughter.

Dubai Police told local media his death was: 'Not suspicious.'

We inmates never did find out what killed Peter. A drug overdose or lack of insulin, who knows?

We were very sceptical about why Peter died, and to this day the cause of his untimely death isn't in the public arena.

Prison diary, December 22nd 2011: There was a fight in the yard last week. Five Emiratis kicked another man's head in. We were locked in for five days. Things back to normal now.

Prison diary, December 23rd 2011: Cellmate Martin has been 'asleep' for about two days suffering from depression. I saw him get up for just thirty minutes yesterday.

Not long after Peter died, I got a message to ring my wife Susan urgently. She told me to call my sister, Magda, at her home in Wales.

Magada told me dad was dead. They'd found him in his favorite chair.

I had a strong connection to my adoptive dad Ken Margetts. He knew I was in jail and we talked by phone about once a month. His wife, my adoptive mom, had already passed away when I'd been at university and he lived alone.

Dad had a good innings as they say, dying of old age in his late eighties.

He'd been a fantastic role model. A former British Army veteran he'd sparked my interest in all sports, especially cycling.

His death was a serious blow and caused me a few dark days.

Fellow inmates were like family members confined in a small

cell so there was plenty of squabbling over nothing really; the type of bickering you might have between siblings.

I'd had a few run-ins with one guy who was a British crime boss, whom I won't name, but he showed me a huge amount of compassion when I became very low over dad's death.

Who would have thought a hard man with such a violent past would have turned out to be a shoulder to cry on? You live and learn.

I wanted to go to dad's funeral in the UK and asked my lawyer Abdullah to get permission, on the basis they could only say no.

To my amazement he got in touch with Dubai's Ruler Sheikh Mohammed direct and asked if I could be released on a temporary basis to travel to Wales.

In passing, can you imagine a lawyer in the UK asking one of the British royals if a nondescript prisoner could go to his dad's funeral?

Word came back from the Palace: I would have been let out temporarily if the funeral had been in the UAE, but a trip to Wales? No way.

At least I asked!

10

Hunger strike

Prison diary, January 8th 2012: I go to court again today. But lawyer Abdullah didn't turn u and the judge gave me an extra three months. Abdullah apologised saying he thought the hearing was next day. Impossible. Court's closed on Fridays Abdullah

Prison diary, January 12th 2012: Learning Spanish. My law studies were going reasonably well. I've covered contract and tort so far. Vaguely thinking about doing a PhD in law. Might as well use jail time for something useful.

It was early 2012. I'd been in prison three years. Yes, count them: one, two, three fucking years. When I was first arrested, I thought I'd be released that night or the following morning. I often reflected on how naive I'd been and how cruel was Dubai's legal system.

Since I'd been behind bars my wife, Susan, and daughter Olivia had started a new life in Europe. Olivia was growing up fast, and it grieved me deeply I wasn't there for her like any other loving dad. Also, my own father had died, and I'd not been able to attend his funeral. Meanwhile, as jail conditions deteriorated, I'd hit a brick wall in terms of getting out of there.

Having to serve forty-two years was becoming a serious reality.

Not that the legal process wasn't rumbling on. The court system was treating every dud check I'd written as a separate offense, in other words: forty-two checks each assigned a different court hearing.

I'd appeared in court close to 300 times; at least twice a week on average; every occasion no more than ten minutes in front of a judge in what I described earlier as a legal madhouse.

Sometimes my lawyer Abdullah turned up, other times he sent an assistant, but on most occasions, I was on own in proceedings conducted entirely in Arabic, and maddeningly I sometimes had a case against me in different courts at the same time on the same day.

The prison guards were as helpful as they could be, but they often got mixed up with the court numbers and took me to, perhaps, court seven when I should have been in five. If I wasn't there, the case went ahead anyway with the judge angry I wasn't in court.

On the rare occasions the planets aligned and the guards got me to the correct court on the right date on time, the judge who'd seen me multiple times before, would usually frown at me with disdain as if to say: 'Dear God, not you again!'

Some judges and prosecutors were real bastards.

I recall an early appearance before Prosecutor Al-M. an arrogant prick at the best of times who wore braces like a hood in the movie *The Goodfellas*.

The court room back and forth went:

Prosecutor Al-M.: 'Forty-two people have filed fraud cases against you, Margetts.' (At least he got my name right!)

Me: 'But, sir, the security checks I signed are post-dated.'

'They've not passed their due dates yet.'

'How can this be fraud?'

Prosecutor Al-M.: 'It doesn't matter. I've decided it's fraud. You're guilty. You, have the pilots' money, give them their money back.'

Me: 'No, I don't have the pilots' money, what's left is in an escrow account. The pilots know most of their money was spent building the apartment block they invested in.'

'The Dubai property crash made the properties virtually worthless. The buyers pulled out. It wasn't my fault my firm went bust.'

Prosecutor Al-M.: 'Margetts, you signed dud checks, you're a fraudster.'

'Good-bye, Margetts.'

'Return him to jail guards.'

As you can appreciate from that encounter every court appearance, especially with no lawyer present, was a farce; at best: a legal lucky dip and it was traumatic in other ways.

From early morning I spent the whole day handcuffed and confined to an underground holding pen beneath the courts fretting over when my case was on, whether I'd be able to pick my name out from the crackling Tannoy announcements and would Abdullah my lawyer be there? Did the guards know which court I was in?

Amid the discomfort of the noise and press of bodies I was squeezed in with hundreds of sweat-soaked Asian and Arab men, often chain smoking; shoplifters, fraudsters, rapists, drug warlords and murderers

Going to court also meant a whole day without food as there was none at the courthouse and we usually weren't bussed back to jail until after the last meal sitting,

Hell, doesn't begin, to describe, my futile years and years, of appearances at Dubai's Court of Misdemeanors.

Looking back, I don't know how I managed to stay sane.

Prison diary, February 14th 2012: Two rules in here: first, trust no one. Second, if you trust someone, wait for them to let you down.

Prison diary, February 16th 2012 :Have realised it's dog-eat-dog in here. When it comes down to it every prisoner is on his own.

With effectively a life sentence to serve and no way out of my nightmare I tried not to mull things too much or my brain would have exploded.

Every morning I thanked God I was lucky enough to exercise, or I might have seriously harmed someone, and Lord knows there were plenty of obnoxious twats to take my frustration and anger out on. There was a German in our cell for example who broke wind so often we called him: Mr. Farty Pants!

Of course, I wasn't the only prisoner suffering mentally. By early 2012 there were thousands of so-called check cases behind bars in Dubai Central; mostly Westerners and Asian businessmen, intelligent entrepreneurs, all yearning to be reunited with families and hoping like hell some white knight would drop by and declare: 'Sorry chaps. This was all a dreadful mistake, you're free to go.'

Until that unlikely event happened we Brits had expected a lot more effort from our government to get us released, but as the months and years rolled by it became clear the rock-solid diplomatic and economic ties between the UK and UAE were, on balance, more of a hindrance than a benefit.

Yes, British Embassy officials indulged us by arranging jail visits, they listened to our complaints, arranged doctors or dental treatment. However, it was little more than lip service really. And there was a reason for that.

'We want to sell the UAE a multi-billion-pound arms package. Don't rock the boat!'

'Look old boy, don't do anything upset Sheikh Mo, there's a good chap,' were the lines I imagined mandarins at the Foreign Office in London pedalled all the time; principles which British Embassy officials in Dubai followed slavishly.

To understand the British Foreign Office's policy and why we were effectively brushed under the carpet as pesky irritants, it's worth reflecting on how the three-centuries-old relationship between the two countries had its genesis and development.

Prison diary, February 25th 2012: Was musing over my brother Joe's life. He'd drunk himself to death and I was sitting in a prison cell. What would our mother have thought?

Prison diary, February 26th 2012: We've not been allowed out of our cells for more twenty minutes on Friday and Saturday. I realise how you could really break a man by not letting him see daylight.

Dubai's Al-Maktoum dynasty had its origins in 1833. Tribal elders started signing treaties with the British in return for protection from Royal Navy ships who obligingly blew marauding pirates and tribes hostile to the Maktoums out of the water; gun boat diplomacy combined with a protection racket were the foundation stones of the relationship.

The strong inter-government friendship grew steadily through the twentieth century, during which the first British owned Imperial Airways flying boats began splashing down in Dubai Creek in 1937.

Then came a golden era from 1958 which blossomed after the current ruler's father Sheikh Rashid and a large entourage of princes, princesses and hangers-on were invited for a free two-week stay at London's Savoy Hotel, thanks partly to the generosity of the British government; the highlight of the massive freebie being the Sheikh's first meeting with young Queen Elizabeth II at a military tattoo known as the Royal Tournament.

The British monarch and the Sheikh got on famously; the Sheikh also fell in love with London and especially enjoyed riding the capital's Tube system.

Ties were so strong in the 1970s it surprised no one when, in 1972, The Queen officially inaugurated Dubai's first deep-water port: the Sheikh's brainchild and an enabler for the emirate to join the world's major league in terms of trade.

That special relationship continued after Sheikh Rashid died; some say from a broken heart after his wife passed away. The current Ruler Sheikh Mohammed, who took over from his brother in 2006, shares a strong bond to the queen to this day.

Easy to understand why. The two monarchs have mutual love of horses and horse racing. The Queen is a keen horsewoman and has an encyclopedic knowledge of thoroughbred horse racing. Sheikh Mo. founded the world-renowned Godolphin horse racing stables in England and is often seen at race-courses like Ascot.

But the relationship between the UK and the UAE goes far

beyond horse racing and tea and cupcakes at Windsor Castle.

There's a solid commercial bedrock underpinning these ties.

When I was in jail, the UAE was the UK's fourth biggest export market outside of Europe with trade between the two countries worth around U.S.$15 billion a year.

At the time of writing this book trade rose to U.S.$20 billion, half of that arms sales and dual use equipment like cyber surveillance.

But although I and other check case inmates were an awkward threat to three hundred years of history and 'megabucks' arms and trade deals, we couldn't just sit there and rot.

Dubai had signed an international treaty outlawing cruel and inhuman punishment.

We were suffering. We thought unjustly so.

We had rights and we could be ignored no longer.

It was time to do something drastic and let the world know.

Prison diary, April 25th 2012: I was very down today, I mean, really, down. I realised I was getting more, angry, and short tempered every day. I wondered vaguely whether some savior would get me out, in time for World Cup in 2014 in Brazil. Never, it's not going to happen.

Prison diary, April 26th 2012: We talked about a possible hunger strike by us: the check-case guys. Drugs wing also said they'd join us, in protest at overcrowding.

I can't recall who mentioned it first, but there'd been a lot of gossip on our wing about starting a hunger strike to highlight our plight and force the Dubai authorities to listen. And, as the chatter became more serious, I began stuffing myself with food, just in case!

One Sunday, in late April, I was gossiping with Irishman Chris Reneham and Belgian Ollie Loeb. The pair were very decent business guys in their forties, both check cases and, like me, mentally worn down to breaking point with frustration.

'Go on hunger strike? said Chris, who was eight months into a six-year sentence.

'You know what? I'm going to do it. We've no other choice... we've nothing to lose'

I thought: nothing to lose? Nothing except your life Chris. But I let that one go.

'I'm up for it, too,' Ollie chimed.

For a moment I smiled, only because Ollie's Belgian accent sounded so like the comedy French policeman in the BBC series: 'Allo, Allo!'

Ollie and Chris shook hands and headed to the main office to let the prison governor know they'd be refusing food.

The pair's decision spurred me to follow their lead. My mind made up, I too toddled along to the prison governor Lt. Colonel Al-Hakim's office.

'What's this hunger strike thing all about, Mr. Peter?' Al-Hakim asked, in his usual laconic style.

I liked Al-Hakim. He was five years from retirement, wanted a quiet life and *inshallah:* to enjoy his pension.

'What do you guys want me to do?' he inquired

I explained our demand was simple. We needed him to set up urgent meeting with Dubai's Attorney General Essa Al-Humaidan to ask him to look-into the so-called check cases with a view to reducing sentences.

Al-Hakim knew I was serving forty-two years and had told me he thought the sentence was outrageous.

'Look, Mr. Peter, I'm on your side,' said the Lt. Colonel.

'Please don't go on hunger strike; it'll cause problems.'

I firmly told Al-Hakim the strike was going ahead, however we'd call it off, if we could meet with the Attorney General.

'OK,' he said. 'Leave it to me.'

I knew Al-Hakim would probably keep his word, meanwhile from that day myself, Chris, Ollie and around eighteen other inmates stopped eating, although we agreed to drink liquids.

And so, it began. I must say the first forty-eight hours weren't at all bad. In the first flush of a hunger strike we were buoyed up because, for the first time, we'd effectively taken control of our own destinies and I for one had decided I was prepared to die rather than serve forty-two years in Dubai Central.

But, by the third, and fourth day serious hunger pangs kicked in. I felt myself get weaker by the hour. I heard people say starvation is one of the cruelest ways to die and I began to believe them

On the fifth day I felt an overwhelming primeval urge to hunt for food. Think: stone age caveman wielding a club looking for wild boar.

Six days in: I was seriously wired pacing the cell back and forth like a caged animal. My temperature soared and my urine turned dark brown.

After fourteen days some of the lads had thrown in the towel and started eating again; I can't blame them, it was an extremely tough gig.

But I was among others still holding out and we underwent profound mental and physical changes.

Naturally weight fell off all of us, but the serious hunger pangs subsided and had given way to a sense almost of serenity -a sort of starvation induced Nirvana.

Physically my body had slowed. I noticed my heart rate fell. I was short of breath. My short-term memory played tricks. My speech became slurred.

By the third week I started to sleep much longer as I grew increasingly weaker. Leveraging myself out of my bunk to drink tea and water had become massively painful as my muscles ached. Every move needed so much pre-planning and willpower.

But you know what? My resolve to continue wasn't broken and was boosted further by another dramatic development which, to our delight, made the Dubai authorities squirm like speared eels.

Prison diary, April 1st 2012: Three guys from Georgia were in court today on burglary charges. They'd only been in Dubai three weeks before they were arrested.

Prison diary April 3rd 2012: Taking no food is hell. I decided to go in to radio silence for a few days, just laying on my bed reading. All my cases were swirling around several courts all at the same time. I barely grasped what was going on and my lawyer certainly didn't have a clue.

One of the lads managed to speak to a British newspaper reporter based in Dubai by phone, which really lit a blue touch paper.

From memory it was Hugh Tomlinson of *Times of London*

who wrote the first article. Suddenly we hunger strikers were a big story.

Simeon Kerr penned a piece in the *Financial Times* and the *Daily Telegraph*, *Daily Express* and *The Independent*, all ran with the news.

Then, the international news agency Reuters picked it up followed by the other big agency Associated Press which brought us to world attention.

Suddenly the story of our dramatic protest had taken on a life of its own.

The family of Briton Safi Qurashi, who was in jail and on hunger strike with me, started picketing the UAE Embassy in West London and got themselves on Sky News, the BBC and CNN.

Safi, who was a terrific guy, had been jailed for seven years in 2010 for writing a single bounced check. His family thought that was outrageous and used the international media brilliantly to tell the world.

'It's been a nightmare. For nearly three years it's turned our family upside down, his wife Huma told Sky News:

'Safi used to do everything. But now I've had to sort out the business and look after the children as well as fight to get him released.'

I also was interviewed by several newspapers including the *Daily Express* which wrote:

'In a shambolic show of justice, Margetts was tried before several courts because the bounced checks had been handed in at different police stations.

'It resulted in the farce, of one court convicting him in his

absence, because he was attending another hearing at the same time. He was jailed in 2009 for a total of 42 years.'

'Good stuff,' I thought. I liked the word 'farce' and wondered how it would translate in Arabic.

Another newspaper had tracked down Chris's dad Michael.

'It's a very troublesome time,' said the father from Dublin.

'Chris is very tired and weak. I haven't a clue how long he will carry on. He's very strong-headed.'

Meanwhile more embarrassment for the Dubai Government: the local English language newspaper, *The National*, also gave our hunger strike prominence. In fact, fair play to her, the female reporter from *The National* did a great job printing our grievances in full. I was amazed at her diligence and at The National for publishing the story in a country where the media is semi, state controlled.

But how did the British Government react to its nationals on hunger strike?

When reporters contacted the British Embassy in Dubai, they got a simple, non-committal quote: 'The embassy was aware of the hunger strike and was monitoring the situation.'

Aside from extensive media coverage, which buoyed us up hugely, American hunger striker Zack Shahin also wrote a letter to U.S. President Barak Obama appealing for him to intervene.

Zack's, scrawling, hand-written note, brought diplomats from the U.S. Consulate General's office in Dubai scurrying to the jail and after meeting Zack they released statement: 'We are concerned about Mr. Shahin's health and we are working with officials to monitor his condition.'

Later, speaking to Reuters, Zack pledged to continue refusing food. 'I've been in prison for four-and-a-half years without a judgment. This is inhuman.'

He added poignantly: 'I've told my daughter I'm coming home, even if it's in a box.'

Prison diary, May 1st 2012: Am pleased Dubai is taking a roasting in the media over our hunger strike.

Prison diary, May 13th 2012: Tensions on wing still bad. Finding it hard to write diary.

The effect of international and local media coverage of the hunger strike sent the Dubai authorities running like headless chickens.

At first, they went into denial. Prison governor, Lt. Colonel Al-Hakim, told journalists: 'There's no hunger strike in Dubai Central, absolutely not, everything's OK,' he blustered.

There was more bull from prison boss Brigadier Omar Al-Attar who told local newspapers: 'Rumors of spreading hunger strikes were unfounded.

'We had an issue with just one inmate and that case was resolved.'

He added: 'We sat with that guy yesterday and spoke to him and said, if you go on strike, what will change?

And I think he understood that.'

'Inmates don't need to do such things.'

'Once the court has, made its decision on a man's sentence, what more can you do?'

Of course, Al-Hakim and Al-Attar had lied through their teeth. The hunger strike was very real, and our resolve was even stronger after the recent publicity.

One journo, I won't name, managed to get through to me by phone and said,

'Peter, I know Al-Hakim and others are lying. Don't worry everyone is on your side. I'll keep plugging away with the story.'

I thanked him sincerely for that.

Flat denials weren't the only reaction from Dubai officialdom to our hunger strike.

Al-Hakim ordered all prisoners be punished whether they were on hunger strike or not.

They cranked up the air conditioning until our cells were like freezers. As well as being desperately hungry I, and others, shivered under blankets.

Punishment didn't stop there. No prisoners were allowed out for recreation, which didn't go down well at all.

I could see what prison bosses were doing. I guessed they hoped draconian measures would make other inmates turn against us and force us to quit our protest: classic divide and rule.

Then, Lebanese inmate Tarek Saleh decided to up the ante and he sent a press release to our media contacts saying a hard-core, sixteen inmates in total, including me, had not eaten solid food for more than twenty days and would stop taking all fluids and medication unless our cases were reviewed.

That hardening of our campaign may have been the reason why, over three weeks into the hunger strike, I got a phone call to from the British Embassy to say officials would be stopping by for a little chat.

Earlier I'd asked to see the Ambassador, but he'd declined, and I heard he told a colleague: 'why would I go to a jail to meet a single British prisoner?'

The Embassy visiting party arrived: Vice-Consul Mandy Smith, Syrian born Hibba, a consular official, and a man I guessed was probably from the British overseas secret service MI6.

The spook was entirely unsympathetic: 'Look we're trying to sell them (the UAE) eighty Tornado jets, it's a deal worth billions,' he said.

'There's no reason why they'd give in to you lot while those big deals are on the table for negotiation. They can treat you how they like and get away with it.'

He turned to me with a sneer: 'Mr. Margetts, do you honestly think you really matter to anyone?'

My anger boiled and I might have thumped him at that point, had Mandy not jumped in with this bombshell.

'Peter do you want to see your family?' she said.

Did bears shit in the wood? Of course, I wanted to see my wife, Susan, and daughter Olivia, what a dumb question.

But then I hesitated.

My skin had already turned yellow and the left side of my face had developed a serious twitch. Did I really want my five-year-old to see her daddy in a jail, in prison pyjamas, looking like an extra in a horror movie?

As my mind raced, I also worried about Susan's safety.

She had nothing to do with the pilots' property deal falling through and my company going bust. But, no one played by the rules in Dubai and if this was a trick, and the police arrested Susan at the airport on some trumped-up pretext, that might be a way of forcing me to give up my hunger strike.

Also, the pilots, who, incredibly, thought I had a secret stash of cash hidden somewhere, could use Susan's arrest to force me to falsely confess I still had money.

Mandy must have read my mind.

'Don't worry about Susan and Olivia's safety. They're going to be OK,' she purred reassuringly.

I wondered, had Embassy officials already been working on a visit by Susan and Olivia and got a guarantee from the Dubai authorities nothing bad would happen to them?

I got the distinct impression, they had, however, I gave no firm commitment about Susan and Olivia visiting me.

With those thoughts hanging, Mandy closed the meeting and pleaded with me and the other hunger strikers not to talk to the media again.

'If you keep talking to the press it's not going to help. The Dubai Government hates it. It might make matters worse for you,' she warned.

Afterwards the Embassy put out another bland statement: 'We are aware of the situation involving prisoners and consular officials visited them last Thursday to inform them about the implications of conducting a hunger strike.'

A week later I had got the surprise of my life.

*Prison diary, May 4th 2012: Worst day so far. I feel so weak. I must carry on.

*Prison diary, May 5th 2012: Fantastic to see Susan and Olivia. Love them both so much.

I'd been on hunger strike for a month and was slowly coming to terms with the reality that I was dying.

When I looked in a mirror, I could see fever in my eyes, my facial tic was getting worse and most days and nights I laid on my bunk wondering how painful death was going to be.

Unexpectedly, a week after the visit by Mandy and embassy officials I got a message to go to prison governor Lt. Colonel Al-Hakim's office where I was escorted to a visiting room.

The door opened and to my utter amazement and pure joy Susan and Olivia were sitting there. I stood in the doorway like a statue and just broke down in tears.

Little Olivia ran to my arms shouting: 'Daddy! Daddy!'

It was an unforgettable, mind-blowing moment, marred only by Olivia trying to hand me a chocolate which a female guard had given her to give to me.

'You have to eat, Mr. Peter,' said the guard.

Nice try I thought. I declined the chocolate and the guard took it away when she left the room.

I was then alone with my precious wife and child. I hugged Olivia almost squeezing the life out of her.

How she'd grown. The last time I'd held she was a toddler.

Over the years I worried she'd forgotten me. But, clearly, she hadn't. I was still her daddy.

Then I hugged my wife, Susan, for the first time since 2009.

I felt safe and at peace with the two most important people in my life, although I was the only one shedding tears!

'My God, it's wonderful to see you both. I can't believe you're here,' I blubbed.

They'd both had an eight-hour flight and Olivia snuggled in my arms and began to slumber while Susan and I talked

'Peter, you look like shit, your face is all lopsided, you've lost so much weight,' my wife said, with typical frankness.

'I know Susan, but myself and the other lads have got to do something.'

'It's the only way left to us to pressure them into reviewing our sentences. We can't just rot in jail. At least they're listening to us now.'

Susan gazed at my skinny frame of bone and gristle and at my twitching face.

'Peter, I don't blame you going on hunger strike,' she said.

'You're doing the right thing. I would have done the same. I'm right behind you.'

Refusing food for weeks and all the mental and physical pain that brought had been the toughest ordeal I'd ever faced, and I was incredibly heartened to hear I had my wife's full support.

We continued to chat about this and that; mainly family matters; until, after twenty minutes, the guard returned saying my wife and child had to leave.

My face-to-face with Susan hadn't been easy and there had been one or two awkward silences, especially when she made it clear she thought I was to blame for being in jail in the first place and I'd been: 'a total bastard,' for putting the family through a nightmare.

The other depressing impression I picked up was, our marriage was probably over. She told me she'd been selling some of our possessions and although she'd struggled with being a single parent, she'd clearly made a new and independent life for herself and Olivia.

That said, Susan had assured me whatever happened, I'd always have access to Olivia, if, by any miracle, I was freed.

Susan's backing for my hunger protest had been a huge boost and if the Embassy had hoped a visit by my wife and daughter would make me change my mind and give in, the strategy hadn't worked. Their plan, I'm happy to say, had backfired.

And so, we said our goodbyes with massive hugs and kisses. The pain I felt saying farewell, I cannot describe in words.

Would I see them again? I didn't know.

What was certain: I was pressing on with my hunger strike with my wife's support, but my struggling vital organs would completely shut down soon. I'd die sometime in the next three weeks.

Prison diary, May 30th 2012: My facial tic much worse. I'm worried might have suffered stroke.

Prison diary June 3rd 2012: Prisoners on the drugs wing still on hunger strike. Prison's view is they just want to get access to hospital to get more drugs. But they were on hunger strike about prison conditions. We check case prisoners just want our freedom.

Susan was right. My face had gone lopsided beneath my left eye, my left cheek was twitching like mad and I was wondering if, by not taking food, I'd suffered a small stroke. I'd collapsed in our cell, although had no clear memory of passing out.

Another inmate must have got through to the UK's *Daily Express*, which reported:

'*Mr. Margetts, 48, was rushed to the hospital wing on Wednesday after collapsing through hunger and suffering a stroke. He is able to talk slightly but is drifting in and out of consciousness and is being fed on a drip.*'

'*His health scare highlights once more the barbaric treatment of prisoners in the United Arab Emirates, coming just a year after the death of tourist Lee Brown who was beaten by police guards in Dubai*

On Friday another British prisoner, property developer Safi Qurashi, aged in his 40s, was taken to the hospital wing with a suspected heart attack. He has refused to eat for 45 days in protest at being jailed for seven years for bouncing a check.'

After I'd been stabilised, a doctor in the prison's medical wing gave me an X-ray and an MRI scan. He concluded I needed to see a neurologist.

Prisoners needing hospital treatment were sent in batches of about six to a nearby infirmary in a little van with a metal cage, and so one morning in April, as sick as I was, I joined others for a jolly-boys outing!

Escapes on hospital runs were fairly common, so we were shackled together, and also handcuffed behind our backs before being shoved into the stifling van. Being bound tight like that in a bouncing vehicle was excruciatingly painful.

When we arrived at the hospital, armed guards marched us in like prisoners in an American chain gang. Ordinary folk waiting to be seen by doctors just sat and gaped.

The female Emirati neurologist I was examined by wasn't exactly chatty. Business-like would describe her general mood.

And who can blame her? She had no idea I was in jail for a white-collar crime. Peter Margetts was harmless, but for all she knew I could have been a rapist or a mass killer.

I told her I was on hunger strike. She gave no reaction.

She ordered me to move my facial muscles by closing my eyes, lifting my brow, frowning and showing my teeth.

'You're suffering from Bell's Palsy, Mr. Peter,' she concluded after the brief exam.

'No-one knows what causes this condition. It's probably viral.'

'I think you've picked up a virus in jail and your body, which is in a very weak state, hasn't been able to fight it.'

And that was it. I don't recall her prescribing any treatment and I was shipped back to jail with the others still resolute my hunger strike would continue.

On hearing about my deteriorating medical condition Radha Stirling, of the human rights group Detained in Dubai, weighed in and told reporters: 'I'm extremely saddened that what is effectively a civil matter was treated criminally and has led to Peter's stroke. The pressure of being imprisoned for something so trivial as a bounced check, and the stress induced from being away from his family has caused such a tremendous reaction.'

That was undoubtedly true, but for the first time since the hunger strike began, I was about to hear some good news.

Prison diary, June 5th 2012: Got notice I'd an appointment with the A.G.

Prison diary, June 7th* 2012: Working out how to play the meeting. My brain very fuzzy now.*

I'd got a message prison governor Lt. Colonel Al-Hakim had fixed me up with an appointment to see Dubai's Attorney General, Essa Al-Humaidan, the following week.

I mean, where else in the world could a prisoner ask to see

the country's top law officer, the man in charge of a courts and law enforcement, and get the response: 'sure why not?'

'Now we're motoring,' I muttered to myself. 'He's the head of the legal system and apart from the Ruler himself there's nobody more powerful.'

Given the general looseness of times and dates in that part of the world; most events are judged *inshallah,* by the will of God; so I was amazed the following week the prison van, with me in it, set off to reach Al-Humaidan's downtown Dubai office on the correct day, in good time for the appointment, and, to my greater surprise, a guard who understood how important the meeting was with the Attorney General, wished me: 'Good luck, Mr. Peter!'

Looking as pale and wasted as anyone could be four weeks without food, with a profound facial tic and totally disheveled, I stepped into the Attorney General's plush office suite like one of Dickens' urchins

His office suite had a photograph of the Ruler on the wall, mahogany furniture was shiny and robust, including a massive glass cabinet, huge desk and several, luxury leather chairs.

Hushed male factotums walked around me with trays of steaming tea in little schooner-shaped glasses that came with half-a-dozen teaspoons of sugar heaped at the bottom. Other flunkies had files under their arms; their patent leather shoes making no sound as they criss-crossed the deep shag-pile carpet; heads bowed deferentially to the Attorney General Al-Humaidan, who was lounging in a low-slung chair, the epitome of 'Joe Cool.'

Al-Humaidan was in his early forties, with a paler skin than most Emiratis and with a round, slightly chubby, face and casual smile.

I can usually sum people up within the first thirty seconds of meeting and as we shook hands, I got a positive vibe from the man. He had no airs and graces.

'Now Mr. Peter, how can I help you?' he asked, getting down to business immediately.

Before I could answer him, he followed up: 'You know, as the Attorney General I can fix anything. So, tell me what you need me to do?'

As I began to set out my case in some detail he nodded attentively, but like all Dubai lawyers I'd ever met, he took no notes, just listened.

Getting into my stride, I launched into the main thrust of my argument.

I pointed out to him the multiple check cases against me were being treated separately, each one as a different individual crime. I'd been handed a year in jail for each check which meant I was serving a forty-two-year sentence, and how could that be right?

I'd been studying the law books the embassy had arranged for me. I was able to argue under Dubai law the writing of the entire pack of dud security checks was a stand-alone, single offense attracting at most a three-year jail term.

I'd served four years already, so I should be freed immediately, I argued.

I let that thought sink in for a few moments and then, the killer argument: 'I need my case and those of the other guys on hunger strike sent to the Court of Cassation (Dubai's Supreme Court) for a decision.'

'We're all in the same boat.'

He mulled it over, shuffled some papers on his desk, and said: 'Yes, yes, you're probably right. I'll sort that out for you.'

'Leave it to me.'

'Oh... don't worry about a lawyer, I'll write your application,' he said, getting up, a cue that the meeting was over.

I was flabbergasted.

Not only had I got to see Dubai's top law official with relative ease, but he'd also agreed with me the decision of the lower courts had been wrong and I and others could appeal.

What's more he said he was ready to send the cases to the Supreme Court for a ruling which, from his tone seemed likely to have a positive outcome. He'd even write my application. Happy days!

On my journey back to jail I wondered what could possibly go wrong?!

Answer: lots!

Prison diary, June 16th 2012: Finding it hard to walk.

Prison diary, June 17t 2012: Suspended diary entries. I can't hold a pen properly.

While I and other hunger strikers waited for a Supreme Court hearing date, we went into a sixth week without food, taking only fluids like water and tea. After a good meeting with the Attorney General we sincerely believed what we were doing was going to be worth it, which made our suffering just about bearable.

After not eating for a month-and-a-half I slipped into a mental haze most days and drifted off on mind-trips of my own reminiscing about my early life, the crazy days, the drink, the drugs and madcap adventures like the ill-fated sea voyage with German yachtsman Werner.

In my more lucid moments I also planned all the things I'd do with daughter Olivia once I'd got out of jail. As her dad, I was determined I would be a big part of her life, and already there were several years to make up for.

But those pleasant daydreams vanished, like the morning mist, one day.

You can never keep a secret in Dubai for long and a sneaky Pakistani civil servant in the Attorney General's office got a message to a prisoner in jail with us. He said he'd read a confidential email sent by the A.G. to judges on the Supreme Court bench.

According to our informant the A.G had written that the legal argument of merging each of the prisoners' check cases into one offense didn't fly in his opinion, and the Supreme Court should turn down our application. This meant the reduction of our sentences to three years maximum was out of the window automatically.

'Oh, fuck! oh, fuck!'

I thumped a table in front of the other lads.

'Surely that cannot be true,' I said, trying my best to comprehend the devastating leaked news.

And we were still in denial over the likely verdict as eighteen of us sat on the bus taking us to the Supreme Court a week later.

In fact we were grim faced and as down as we'd ever been. Weak from no food we must have looked like a real bunch of desperados tramping into the highest court in Dubai.

We were so thin our loose-fitting prison pyjama trousers hardly stayed up. It was a miracle they didn't slip down because we were handcuffed and couldn't reach to hold the waistband.

Then when we got to court, yet another blow.

Even though it was our legal application, we weren't allowed in court! We were told Supreme Court judges reviewed evidence sitting alone.

Dubai's legal system, if I can dignify it with that description, really sucked.

After an hour or so a court clerk hurried out and told us the behind-closed-doors hearing was over; the judges had rejected our cases and our sentences stood.

Our creased, bewildered faces and silence on the way back to jail said all that had to be said, and it was during that journey I decided: my hunger strike was over.

I'd pushed myself to the brink of death. And for what?

Another humiliating and crushing blow delivered by a crazy, fucked up legal system. Even the Attorney General had screwed us over.

I didn't know how much more my spirit could take.

As the prison bus drove through the jail entrance I pondered suicide as the only way out.

Prison diary, August 22nd 2012: Guys wandered from cell to cell, saying 'Happy Eid!' or 'Eid Mubarak!' I felt really isolated at time like that. I remembered, this was similar, to the Christian Christmas, and it was best to stay out of the way of people of the Muslim faith. Let them get on and enjoy it.

Prison diary, August 23rd 2012: Billy was snoring and not as loudly as usual because he'd lost weight. Martin would be staying under his sheets for the weekend. Some guys talk all day and sometimes in their sleep. Dave and Martin in jail 4 years and never had a visitor.

As mentioned in an earlier chapter: I'm not a quitter and it dawned on me if I took my life the bastards would have won. Worse still I'd have given up on my family; my darling Olivia in particular.

So, it was time, once again, to knuckle down, stay out of trouble, keep a low profile and get on with my sentence, whilst I sorted out some other way of appealing.

Meanwhile, following the Supreme Court's devastating pronouncement we'd all thrown in the towel and ended our hunger strike.

I'd started to wolf down food again; tons of rice, chicken, sticky sweets, anything that would help me pile on the pounds

I felt glorious nourishment coursing through my veins, like a life force and it was a wonderful feeling, even my facial tic flickered less.

Little by little my body regained strength and within days my health improved so much I was able to resume hammering out laps in the exercise yard; within a few weeks I'd fully regained my memory as the old brain cells kicked in again

I knew Margetts was finally on the mend after my piss turned color from dark brown to a healthy, pale-yellow!

Meanwhile, me and the other hunger-strikers, like American Zak and Irishman Chris, spent some time reflecting on our protest.

We hadn't achieved our goal of getting our sentences cut,

but we'd attracted masses of media coverage along the way. And there'd been other bonuses from our pain and suffering.

I heard through the British Embassy that Prime Minister David Cameron had taken an interest in UK check case prisoners and asked to be kept informed; that news lifted my sprits hugely.

And it wasn't only Downing Street getting on the case.

Because we hunger strikers were from several nations, most of them UAE allies, the Dubai government was feeling the heat from concerned senior politicians across the world.

Prison diary, September 28th 2012: Generally coping but sometimes hit new lows. Last few days were torture. I realised I messed up not only my life but those closest to me.

Prison diary, September 30th 2012: It was getting tense in the cells living with other men 24/7, 365 days a year in forty-degree heat, minimum, is a real test. Am surprised not more fights.

Local newspapers had given our hunger strike story lots of coverage, sparking a national debate in Dubai where pernicious check laws still wreaked havoc.

Job cuts and long construction delays meant expat borrowers, who'd bought apartments at the top of the market, were holding mortgages they couldn't afford, on homes worth up to forty percent less than they'd paid, and their post-dated security checks weren't being honored.

When banks and mortgage companies refused to negotiate, it was safer to pack up and catch the next flight to anywhere before the cops came knocking to take the breadwinner to jail.

I read by 2012 the value of bounced checks in Dubai totalled U.S.$13 billion, according to the Central Bank, ten times the amount in the UK for example.

I can confidently say, as a direct result of our hunger strike, a media lead debate called for a major overhaul of the checks laws.

There was some resistance, although most accepted there needed to be change.

Dubai lawyer Habib Al-Mullah told a newspaper: 'This checks system is rooted in society. To change, you must find an alternative. Until today there is no other alternative.'

He continued: 'But the government shouldn't be responsible for being a debt collector.'

Dubai Police Chief Lt. General Dahi Khalfan also weighed in: 'Pursuing people whose checks bounced was a waste of police time.'

A consensus grew that both creditors and debtors alike, had to be protected. The problem was that Dubai had no fair bankruptcy laws in place, which was ridiculous for a modern city-state where most people paid for their mortgages, rents and cars with post-dated security checks.

As the debate rumbled on Dubai's economists, financiers and lawyers mulled the alternatives.

How about a cash deposit instead of the first check, was one suggestion? That was quickly ruled out.

Checks were still the way forward, according to Abdul Aziz Al-Ghurair, chief executive of Mashreq Bank who told a Dubai conference: 'The checks system today is serving us well and without a holistic system in place it will be a catastrophe for business if it's removed.'

The international bank, HSBC, echoed the same view.

At the same time an Emirati businessman in jail with me, known only by his initials in court as AQ, brought a lawsuit questioning the constitutionality of Dubai's Penal Code.

His lawyer argued: 'The law currently states a person who defaults on a check, with or without criminal intention, can be jailed or fined. Where there was no criminal intent, the case should stay in the civil courts for an arbitrated settlement, on a similar basis to the legal process in Western countries.

People must sign blank checks to rent, borrow, purchase and do business in Dubai. If conditions make it the only method of doing business, the courts must not criminalise non-payment.'

I couldn't have agreed more. I'd had no criminal intent when I wrote the pilots their checks. I was just using an accepted system of making payments with post-dated checks.

As the debate on security checks ebbed and flowed, we inmates were still allowed to make calls to the media.

'How can there be criminal or malicious intent when you write a security check for a credit card and then lose your job?' my Belgian cellmate Ollie Loeb asked a newspaper reporter.

'You can hold our passports, give us a travel ban, do whatever is needed, but we need to get out of jail so we can run our companies and feed our families,' the Belgian businessmen added.

Both myself and other inmates were proud that our hunger strike had sparked a debate in Dubai, and even prouder when we heard there was going to be a dramatic change to the security check system which had caused so much misery.

First, in a move to stop Emiratis falling into debt, and, following a recent census registering all locals, Dubai's banks said they were able to set up a federal credit bureau which would assess a customer's credit worthiness and therefore their ability to write a check that wasn't going to bounce.

Secondly: Central Bank expanded the Debt Settlement Fund for Emiratis, increasing eligibility to those with debts of up to U.S.$1.3 million, to have their personal loans repaid if they'd been jailed or faced trial.

So far so good.

Thirdly, and this was the big one; to mark the religious holiday *Eid Al Adha* in October 2012, a Presidential decree ordered that any Emirati who faced jail for writing a dud check to banks or finance houses would be immune from prosecution.

We held our breath. There was more. The president ordered that check case Emiratis who were currently in jail should be freed!

More than a thousand joyful locals walked out of their cells and headed home to their families.

Don't misunderstand me. I was very happy for them. But it was our hunger strike that brought all this about.

'What about us non-Emiratis, Mr. President? Can't we be freed as well?'

That was the message we asked the British Embassy to convey to the UAE government.

Answer came there none.

11

Gracias amigo

Prison diary, November 5th 2012: I could feel a fight brewing. The Germans were 'pissy' because the phones were down. Dirk, the German, was in line to be beaten senseless by Iranian Ali, local rapist. I played football but a couple of Arab 'nutters', who hated Europeans, they nearly broke my wrist -they wanted to smash my leg

Prison diary, November 8th 2012: I've started to have nightmares which I've never had before. My father is strangling me. Bully looks in. He says I was shouting, 'no, no, no' in the night. Bully tells me, 'Don't worry no-one will touch you.'

As you'll have gathered, my years in Dubai Central had, so far, been an unimaginable ordeal, but the roller coaster journey wasn't all bad.

The cons I mixed with were from all walks of life; business executives like myself, hardened criminals such as bank robbers, rapists, murders and drug warlords; some very rough diamonds indeed, but most had redeeming features if you looked for them such as, a great sense of humor, an ability to make the best of it and so on.

Some guys I spent time with will remain friends for life; more about them in the last pages.

My other positive takeaway from an otherwise horrific episode in my life, was the hundreds of hours of enjoyment I spent playing football and the team camaraderie which went with it.

To be frank, had I not been able to kick a ball around and join in team games, I'd have lost my mind.

During my early days behind bars inmates were allowed exercise twice a day. That was cut to an hour a day, or sometimes not at all, when prison overcrowding started or during our hunger strike.

'*Riyada, riyada, riyada,* sport, sport, sport,' the guards used to cry.

The electronic gates would click open and we'd run out like kids in a school playground at breaktime, relieved to be out of the confines of a prison cell.

Although the jail boasted a weights room and basketball hoops, football was really the only show in town, so much so, virtually every inmate played, be they young, or old-timers like me.

Even reluctant ones, the, 'I hate football' crowd, were shoved kicking and screaming into goal.

And if that failed, they watched from the sideline.

When I first arrived at Dubai Central, organized footie matches were mostly *ad hoc* and the only prisoners who formed actual teams were the Emiratis. The locals always saw themselves as a superior race and anyone of another nationality was kicked off their precious, concrete pitch in short order.

Then, when they realised, guys like me, had footballing

skills, the Emiratis not only consented to other nationalities playing against them, but also agreed they could form sides of their own.

Some prison inmates were real hotshots. A handful were former professional players, including a French Algerian, midfielder who used to play for the top French club, Lille, and minor English teams like Bristol City.

Matches on the concrete pitch were neither played by the FIFA rule book, nor were they ever likely to be. The pitch was a place where frustrations, about being in jail, were vented, so brutal fouls were commonplace and the intensity of bad tackles was often influenced by the international political scene.

When the British Air Force bombed the crap out of Libya, or the UK government sided with Israel in a hot war with Gaza's Palestinians, or the Western coalition backed a U.S. cruise missile attack on a Syrian Air Force base, that's when we Brits faced a backlash. It could include a potentially leg-breaking assault, a fist in the face or a heavy kick in the nuts. The Arabs saw it as payback time.

I was playing in goal once and an angry Algerian kicked a ball at me so hard from about twenty feet my left middle finger snapped back ninety degrees. The pain from my twisted digit was excruciating, until a Nigerian lad leapt forward, yanked my finger back into place and shouted: 'play on!'

Although a football match in Dubai Central was, undoubtedly, robustly, competitive; if I can put it that way. It was also a great leveler.

You could be a mass murderer, an East European mafia boss, a diamond thief or just a bad debtor; nobody cared. Your status in the hierarchy of inmates rested on how many goals you hammered in, how many guys from the other team you could outrun or successfully tackle.

I'm going to shamelessly blow my own trumpet here and say I was very fit for my age. Often my side won the game, simply thanks to my skill as a striker. I have no doubt kudos earned on the football pitch, when hundreds of hardened criminals watched in admiration, saved me from a random beating.

Knock the crowd dead on the football pitch and you walked tall in Dubai Central.

'Nice game, Peter, you good player,' said one admiring East European mafia boss, putting his tattooed arms around my shoulder with affection, instead of thumping me.

In the early days none of the teams we'd formed had names and I decided to do something about that.

I thought it might motivate the lads in our wing to have a team name; give them some team pride, especially when they faced a side of convicted African murderers on a sweltering afternoon.

So, I came up with the idea of names based on crimes committed.

There was only one possible name for us: Bounced Checks United! I was proud of that one.

Other inmates went along with the naming idea and thereafter Bounced Checks United began playing against teams like: Murder One, Murder Two, Rape One and Drugs One, Two, Three, Four and Five, and so on.

I'm proud to say Bounced Checks United was often top of Dubai Central's makeshift football league and I'd be overly modest if I didn't say, even at my age, and playing amongst guys who were twenty-years younger, I was a bit of a star.

An ace striker in my forties! Who'd have thought it?

But, at this point I must describe of one of most surreal incidents during my time in Dubai Central involving one of the most famous footballers on the planet -a god in fact!

Prison diary, October 2nd 2012: Safi, a British guy, one of the checks cases, got articles in the Daily Telegraph and The Guardian. *He'd been successful in getting an application to be released heard by the Ruler's Court. I wished him luck.*

Prison diary, October 1st 2012: I couldn't even bring myself to talk to my family. There was a flood. Someone let the fire sprinklers off.

Given there were so many nationalities banged up in Dubai Central and football was such a big part of our lives, prison bosses came up with the idea of a jail World Cup.

Staggeringly, the Dubai Government had apparently stumped up prize money of U.S.$55,000 to be divided between the winning team, the best player, goalkeeper and striker.

Inmates were extremely sceptical that any cash would be handed over, in actuality; however I digress.

Not only was there a hefty money prize, we learned that the real World Cup football legend, Diego Maradona, who coached Dubai's Al-Wasl F.C., would be presenting the freaking trophy!

It had been more than twenty years since Maradona held the World Cup aloft, but his plan to drop in to Dubai Central was so bizarre, so surreal, we'd surely be forgiven for not quite believing it.

Despite our doubts anything was possible in that prison madhouse and as the date of the Hand of God legend's arrival approached Dubai Central rocked to its foundations with anticipation

Twelve teams competed in the Dubai Central World Cup, with prisoners representing the UAE, Iran, UK, India, Mexico, Cameroon, Egypt, Pakistan, The Philippines, Vietnam, Nigeria and Ivory Coast. Each team had seven players and a goalkeeper.

In the run-up to the final, I was in the UK side and we made it to the quarter-finals, but were knocked out by the UAE.

Then UAE went on to play Nigeria in the semis and lost.

UAE government officials were extremely pissed their side had been crushed, so they were ordered to play again, and again, in the hope they'd win!

It was not to be. The UAE side had several prisoners who were hardened junkies and no match for the towering, ultra-fit Nigerians.

So came the day of the final, with Nigeria set to slug it out with another strong African side, Cameroon.

To our amazement a police convoy, with blue lights flashing, swept into the jail, bringing with them with a diminutive civilian in a track suit and with distinctive curly black hair; none other than Maradona himself!

I happened to be in the Visitors' center, chatting to some Colombian prisoners, when the Argentinian football genius strode in and flashed a massive smile. At first, we watched open-jawed.

The Colombians shouted a few *holas* and other Spanish phrases I didn't understand and Maradona, as cool as anything, waved back. Then, he gave a hearty thumbs up to us all.

Being a keen football player and fan of the game all my life, I was completely starstruck by his charisma and amazing warmth.

And yes, I pinched myself. How fucking surreal? There I was, locked up in Dubai Central, hobnobbing with one of the greatest football players that ever lived. You couldn't have made it up.

Maradona shunned any police protection and made his way out to the concrete pitch for the jail World Cup, to the delight of more than a thousand cheering prisoners.

The place was banging with excitement and one group of inmates carried a banner reading: 'Greeting and thanks to Diego Maradona, welcome to our home.'

'Many people struggle to try to meet this guy in person,' said thirty-seven-year-old prisoner Enos Ogada, a Nigerian who managed the Ivory Coast team.

'It is a football lover's dream. For him to come to us, it was a prayer answered'

After the cheering died Maradona had the crowd in his hand as he stepped to the podium and addressed us.

Perhaps drawing on his own brushes with the law, which included a drugs rap and an assault charge for shooting a journalist with an air rifle, Maradona said: 'We all might commit mistakes, but it is possible, after getting out, to look to our lives and future in a better light.'

Assisted by an inmate who translated, Maradona went on: 'And there is no better way than football to give a better feeling of the future.'

What a great message, I thought. There was a football hero, admired by every prisoner, telling us it was possible to turn our lives around, meanwhile, we inmates serving time, however unjust, should enjoy the beautiful game to lift our spirits.

Nice one, Diego!

After his uplifting speech we were forced to endure a horse dancing show and mock demonstrations by police of their fugitive tracking skills using dogs, which frankly received a muted reception from inmates.

Then, Maradona stepped onto the pitch to kick off for the final.

Nigeria roared ahead and scored in the first five minutes and went on to beat Cameroon, 'One-Nil,' to huge cheers. It had been a fair win.

After accepting the jail World Cup from Maradona, James Josephat, the captain of the Nigerian team, who was serving two years, spoke of the bitter-sweet moment.

He said: 'We appreciate all the efforts, and it is good Maradona is with us, but we are still not happy for being here. We want to be given another chance.'

Another Nigerian player, Andrew Eshio said: 'We have lost our lives here. Some of us have lost wives, children, fathers and mothers. They've died whilst we've been in here. We're begging for a second chance.'

Those poignant comments were a timely reminder of some of the injustices of the Dubai legal system.

Sure, some members of the Nigerian team who'd just dazzled us on the pitch, were hardened criminals, rightly convicted and properly in jail for heinous crimes like murder and armed robbery. But, I knew enough to assume some had been found guilty on the flimsiest of evidence or had been handed vastly over-long sentences by corrupt judges, a fate suffered by many Africans who, generally speaking, were treated abominably in Dubai, whether they were criminals or not.

As for Maradona? What an amazing guy! The fifth of eight

children born in a slum near Buenos Aires, who grew to be a megastar on the sporting world stage. He'd shown great modesty and humility that hot afternoon at Dubai Central. It had been an incredible event.

He'd lifted spirits and restored hope to prisoners who had none.

'Gracias, mi amigo!'

12

Death in the afternoon

Prison diary, August 13th 2013: Shown a cutting where a reporter for The Gulf News *(local UAE newspaper) described Dubai Central jail as 'hotel' for prisoners! A HOTEL? The article talks about murderers learning trades in a workshop. It says there's a library with 4500 books. Yes, Gulf News, 4,400 of them are The Koran!*

Prison diary August 15th 2013: Resolved to write to the Gulf News with the truth about Dubai Central. My cell is a room 32 ft square housing 6 men in bunks. We have no tables, no chairs and only our bunks to sit on. There are 60 men penned in our wing. We have access to a phone for 2 hours a week. We have one TV and one table tennis table. Nothing else.

Although physical violence between inmates, attacks by guards on inmates, and assaults by prisoners on guards, were part and parcel of everyday life in Dubai Central, there was one grisly and blood-soaked killing which shook the place to its foundations.

Let me give you some background and introduce to you Emirati mobster Ayyoub Abdul Rida. And let's be personal and call him Ayyoub.

He was in jail the same time as me. I usually saw him at exercise time. I kept my distance, as I did from most prison dons.

He and bunch of Chechen thugs, who'd been imprisoned for armed robbery, had a protection racket going, so it was safer to stay clear of them.

Ayyoub wasn't your typical crime boss. He was a short little runt; sinewy, not an ounce of fat and just five feet five inches tall, if that. Not exactly Tony Soprano!

On the rare occasions I saw him at close quarters, I guessed he was in his early forties, probably of Persian stock originally, with an adolescent's whispy, black beard and moustache. Ayyoub had a face only a mother could love, think: bulldog chewing a wasp.

Despite his short stature beating someone to a pulp was all in a day's work. However, his speciality was arson, and not just his rival's properties. He once torched a Dubai police station, in a fit of peak

His 'nom de guerre' in Dubai's underworld was, Ayoub the Burned, so-called because, whilst he was fire-bombing some poor sod's downtown office, he missed his footing and set his *dishdasha* and himself alight!

Oh dear, what a shame!

Dubai's mobsters were no different to crime families in other parts of the world. They were always battling for turf.

So, you had Ayoub's clan and their nemesis in the city's darker quarters; the Raizan family, fighting over various drug, extortion and prostitution rackets.

During a punch-up with one of the Raizans, Ayyoub had sliced his opponent's finger off with a knife. Not surprisingly, the Raizans were pissed that one of their soldiers had lost a pinkie, so there was a score to settle.

And by pure kismet, the showdown was in Dubai Central when fatefully Ayyoub and top members of the Raizan gang, Mohammed Raizan and his little shit of a brother; a mouthy waste of space; found themselves under the same roof.

Prison diary, August 16th 2013: Long weekend and no reading, because we had no lights in the cell.

Prison diary, August 17th 2013: There was a young Brit kid brought in today for stealing cars. He was well educated from a wealthy background. They gave him 2 years for stealing one car. He stole many cars, so he'll be here for a long time.

Given there was a score to settle Ayyoub had sensibly been shackled in solitary for his own protection.

But unexpectedly he was released to a general wing when, coincidentally, jail governor Lt. Colonel Al-Hakim was on vacation; a move which raised eyebrows at the time and prompted prison gossips to speculate that Ayyoub was being set up to be 'whacked.'

Fast forward to around five p.m. on Sunday, August 20. The worst of the Gulf's blistering heat had subsided for the day and me and pal Youssif, trotted to the exercise yard. Our plan: to pound out fifty laps.

As soon as we reached the yard, we sensed something bad was about to kick off; imagine a classic Spaghetti Western stand-off, but without the tumbleweed.

In one corner of the exercise yard were Ayyoub's protection racket associates: the Chechens, led by a cocky bastard called Gelani.

In another corner, Ayyoub's bitter rivals Mohammed Raizan, his brother, and a couple of Emirati sidekicks, hell-bent on avenging the finger slicing incident

I watched the two rival gangs eyeing each other and snarling like pitbulls, but there was no still no sign of Ayyoub.

A nervous, young prison guard, who was supposed to be keeping an eye on inmates, suddenly made himself scarce.

Then, one of the Chechens yelled across the yard at Youssif and me: 'Get the fuck out of here. Go on. Fuck off!'

We didn't need telling twice.

As we turned on our heels, Ayyoub suddenly burst out from a wing of the jail and whistled past us brandishing a weapon that glistened in sun. His narrowed eyes burned with hate. In my diary entry I described him as being like a 'Tasmanian Devil'!

He rushed, as fast as his short legs could carry him, toward the Raizan brothers who had their backs turned. Ayyoub plunged his homemade knife into the older Raizan's back and stabbed him like he was possessed by demons. I'd never witnessed such fury.

As Ayyoub slashed the torsos of other Raizan gang members my lasting memory will always be the rash of crimson blood stains suddenly mushrooming on the victims' white shirts from every brutal strike from Ayyoub's glistening blade.

Ayyoub's bloody assault on the Raizan brothers had been the cue for tens of others; Chechens and East Europeans; to rush into the yard where, suddenly, there was a mass brawl underway, without a guard in sight.

Youssif and I dashed for our lives into one of the main blocks. We wanted no part in the mayhem unfolding in the yard, but we stayed within earshot.

As minutes passed the sounds of battle eventually stopped.

When I thought the coast was clear my friend, Belgian Ollie Loeb and I nervously returned to the exercise yard and discovered the melee had shifted to an upper wing in an adjoining prison block. But that fight eventually ended in eerie silence.

Thinking it was over, Ollie and I wandered down a corridor daubed with splashes of blood. The two of us nearly gagged from the sickly scent of gore.

'Have you heard?' yelled another inmate coming the other way.

'Heard what?'

'Ayyoub's dead.'

'He's in that cell on the left down there,' cried another prisoner pointing down the corridor.

'My parents were both doctors. I'll go take a look,' said Ollie, rather incongruously, and disappeared into one of the cells. I waited for him to report back.

A minute or so later a white-faced Ollie returned, shaken to the core by what he'd seen.

'Is Ayoub really dead?' I asked.

'Very fucking dead,' whispered Ollie.

He then described Ayoub's brutalised body in grim detail. Ollie said the midget gangster had been stabbed multiple times. No part of his body had been spared. His opponents had sliced off one his ears, gouged out both his eyes and, with echoes of Jack the Ripper, they'd slit his stomach open and exposed his innards.

As soon as Ollie finished his horrific description, we both decided to get the fuck out of there and fled back to our wing.

Dubai's elite national security force swarmed into Dubai Central, eventually, but it took them about three hours to regain control of the jail.

The first thing they did was line prisoners up in corridors for a head count and then we were locked up twenty-four hours.

Ayyoub's savage murder had been a huge embarrassment to the Dubai Government which routinely used local media to boast how wonderfully safe and educational the jail was: 'a model, caring prison, which released reformed characters back into the wider world,' so the mantra ran.

The post-murder crackdown continued for six weeks and we were only let out of our cells for three meals a day and court visits. Otherwise we were locked up around the clock.

And, like the punishment they meted out when we went on hunger strike, prison bosses cranked up the air conditioning to full blast, so we were forced to sit and shiver in our icebox cells, wrapped in blankets. Some elderly inmates almost died from hypothermia

Prison diary, August 21st 2013: I met an inmate with the poshest voice I've ever heard. He's a British born Indian from Stafford. He regaled me with tales of jetting around the world and his wine collection!

Prison diary, August 22nd 2013: Sad to hear Samir my friend killed himself within a week of being released.

Ayyoub the Burned's assailants eventually ended up in court where a prosecutor revealed the mobster had died from forty stabs wounds caused by makeshift knifes and sharpened wooden sticks. The coup de grâce had been explosive kicks to the head which had smashed his skull.

At the trial Dubai's Criminal Court was ringed by riot police in case Ayyoub's mobster pals attempted to exact their own justice on the eighteen inmates in the dock who'd been charged with pre-meditated murder and faced the death penalty if found guilty

In court more details of Ayyoub's brutal murder emerged. A police witness revealed the mobster: 'had stab wounds on every part of his body.'

Another witness, an inmate, said some defendants had formed a circle to prevent prison guards getting near to stop the final, gruesome act of killing.

'When a prison guard tried to stop them, they threatened to beat him up,' said the witness

In a case which was clearly a slam dunk in terms of who was guilty, to everyone's astonishment all defendants were acquitted. An appeal court upheld the acquittal.

Prosecutors then took the case to Dubai's Supreme Court to try to secure a conviction.

And again, the defendants were acquitted,

Why? Because in the Supreme Court judges' opinion the lower court had correctly decided that poor quality CCTV recordings of the fight failed to show conclusively the facial features of those who participated in the murder. Therefore, it was impossible for police, prosecution and forensic experts to confidently identify the attackers or, crucially, who killed Ayyoub.

There was a further defeat for prosecutors.

Five other defendants, this time members of Ayyoub's gang,

known in court by their initials as ZS, twenty seven, from Georgia, PK, aged thirty two, SE, twenty nine, and JP, forty, both Russian, and EM, thirty one, from Kyrgyzstan, were charged with attempted murder over an earlier fight.

They were also acquitted.

So, nobody was brought to book, not for Ayyoub's slaying and none of his gang involved in a previous attack.

The only sacking we heard about, was a police corporal who unwittingly opened a prison gate to let a forty-strong mob of inmates join the battle that ended in Ayyoub the Burned getting topped.

To this day Ayyoub's clan and the Raizan mob remain bitter enemies.

13

Sheikh Mo

Prison diary, September 10th 2013: Just realized, I haven't worn shoes, or driven a car, for over four years.

Prison diary, September 12th 2013: The court merry-go-round goes on with hearings on the 3rd, the 8th, the 14th, the 27th. Been to court hundreds of times in the last four years. My character is really changing. I'm desperately scared of what's happening to me.

As prison life returned to normal, after the murder of mob boss Ayyoub, I pledged to step up efforts to try to get an early release.

My strategy also included keeping my nose clean, maintaining a low profile, avoiding any altercations and generally being no trouble to guards or anyone else.

But, even with my good behavior, every escape route out of jail seemed blocked. The local lawyers I'd hired were useless, a hunger strike had brought my plight to Downing Street's attention, but had done nothing to secure my freedom. I was losing all hope.

Worse still, I was changing a person. I began not to trust anyone, even the lads in my cell; it felt like I was retreating into my own little shell.

Then, quite unexpectedly, the UK charity, Prisoners Abroad got in touch.

They'd asked London-based lawyer and journalist John Cookson, the co-author of this book, to travel to meet me in jail to see what could be done. For the first time in four years an outside organisation had intervened to help me. Hallelujah!

We met and John immediately agreed to work on a pro-bono basis.

John had lived and worked in the Middle East for the previous twenty years, he was fluent in Arabic, and he realised, as I did, if the Supreme Court had rejected my submission for a sentence reduction and the hunger strike had moved no one, the remaining option had to be action at the highest government level in London and Abu Dhabi.

Unlike my Emirati lawyers I was gratified to see John took reams of notes during our first meeting and promised he'd take things forward by contacting my new Member of Parliament, Zac Goldsmith, to shake things up a bit. Then, John returned to London.

I knew Zac was debonair, his family was 'old money,' as we say in the UK and was made Lord Goldsmith of Richmond in January 2020 so he could stay in Boris Johnson's government after being defeated in a general election, but I had to Google him to find out more.

Educated at Eton College, Zac was son of billionaire businessman and financier Sir James Goldsmith, a fabulously wealthy tycoon, allegedly the inspiration for the fictional character Sir Larry Wildman in the 1987 Hollywood blockbuster *Wall Street*. I read Zac's interests included backgammon, poker, and he was mad about the game of cricket.

Zac's well-known siblings included sister Jemima, who'd been married to the Pakistan cricketer Imran Khan.

His mother was Lady Annabel Goldsmith, a famous London socialite, known for her sense of humor, down to earth personality and love of children and dogs. Swanky Annabel's nightclub in London's Mayfair was named after her.

It was all a bit dazzling to be honest for a humble lad like me, but I recall thinking: if anyone can get me out it's Zac, ably assisted of course by John and the friend I mentioned in an earlier chapter Liverpool-based barrister Richard Gray, who'd also offered his services free on a no win, no fee basis in a civil court case.

After John returned to London, he and Richard pulled together a legal argument on why I should be set free and arranged a meeting with Zac to make a presentation on my behalf.

The bullet-point presentation went something like:

1. My crime of writing forty-two bounced checks was, actually, one single offense which carried a maximum sentence of three-years. John and Richard argued the Dubai courts had been wrong, as a matter of law, to treat each check as a single offence.

2. If point one was accepted, John and Richard argued I should be freed immediately because I'd already served four years.

3. Point three was real lawyers' stuff: they argued that locking someone in his mid-forties for forty-two years was effectively a life sentence and was a 'cruel and inhuman

punishment' contrary to international human rights law.

The UAE wasn't a signatory to the UN Charter on Human Rights, but Abu Dhabi had signed 1992 Arab Charter and the Cairo Declaration, which in terms of content was pretty much the same as the UN treaty

Zac took the legal advice on board and wrote to Foreign Office Minister Alistair Burt MP, who reported to Foreign Secretary William Hague, asking for my case to be raised at what were called inter-governmental task-force meetings held on a regular basis in Abu Dhabi and London.

John also wrote directly to Alistair Burt along the same lines, as back up.

I couldn't have asked for more. Team Margetts settled back and waited for some reaction from on high.

Prison diary, November 2nd 2013: We were punished today because some guys had gone to breakfast without waiting to be called. Vengeance was swift. Exercise yard out of bounds, packs of cards removed, no access to the telephone.

Prison diary, November 5th 2013: This week has been very stressful and words can't describe how frustrating these futile court visits are. I'm going to court at least 2 times a week for an alleged offense that wouldn't be a crime anywhere else.

Some months passed and, I learned that, thanks to the persistence of my MP, Zac Goldsmith, the UK Foreign Minister, Alistair Burt, had regularly raised my case with his opposite number in the UAE government.

I received letters and snippets of information from solicitor John Cookson saying there'd been talk of me being transferred to a UK jail to finish my sentence.

But that was bittersweet. Yes, I'd be serving time in England, however what about the forty-two-year prison term?

I needed to get that reduced and there was one other avenue open to me: an appeal directly to Dubai Ruler, Sheikh Mohammed.

Although Dubai may have the trappings of stable government, backed by one of the best armed militaries in the world and a shadowy secret service known as the *mukhabarat*, the reality is: Dubai is Sheikh Mohammed, and Sheikh Mohammed is Dubai.

No one in Dubai's military, forces of law and order, government or local commerce even farted without his say-so, and one of the symbols of the Sheikh's omnipotence is the Ruler's Court, headquartered in an imposing, white marble complex on the banks of Dubai Creek, complete with massive mosque and towering minaret.

The Ruler's Court considers around three hundred cases a year and it's open for any prisoner to put in an appeal as a last roll of the dice after all other legal options have been exhausted. So, after being slapped down by the Supreme Court for a sentence reduction, I'd decided to throw myself on the Ruler's mercy, on the basis that, I had nothing to lose!

I got hold of the application forms and then settled down to pen an erudite and compelling appeal, but first I mulled over the character of the man I was writing to: Sheikh Mohammed.

His father Sheikh Rashid had a vision to turn Dubai into a global city and his son drove the dream forward by establishing the mega-wealthy and government owned, corporate behemoths: Emirates Airline, DP World, and the Jumeirah Group.

Sheikh Mo. is enormously driven. He's overseen numerous other major projects including a technology park and a free economic zone, Dubai Internet City, Dubai Media City, Dubai International Finance Center, the Palm Islands and the fantastic, seven-star Burj Al Arab hotel.

He was also the visionary and driving force behind the construction of the astonishing Burj Al-Khalifa tower; at almost, a kilometre high, it's currently the tallest building in the world

In his book Dubai, author Jim Krane wrote this accolade to Sheikh Mo: *'a man's man, with the entrepreneurship bravado of Richard Branson, the city building prowess of Robert Moses and the social engineering ambition of Ataturk.'*

And Paul Bagatelas, Director of the Carlyle Group in Dubai weighed in: *'he's a cross between Teddy Roosevelt, the big game hunter who represented emerging America, and Bill Gates, whose personality is inseparable from his personality.'*

As part of my research into Sheikh Mohammed Bin Rashid Al Maktoum, I discovered he was born on July 15th, 1949 and as well as being the Ruler of Dubai he's the UAE's Vice President and Prime Minister.

He had an extraordinary childhood.

His father, Sheikh Rashid, encouraged young Mohammed to embrace the family's bedouin roots and packed him off on desert camping trips where he was taught to hunt gazelle.

During his character building sojourns in the desert, tribal elders toughened him up by shoving live scorpions into his bed as he slept!

They weren't adult scorpions, but still bit him fiercely. I'm told the bite from a young scorpion feels like a wasp sting.

The idea of torturing him was to build his body's resistance up to scorpion venom and to teach him how to handle pain, according the Sheikh's own autobiography: My Story

In his teens, like so many Middle Eastern leaders, he was sent off to the UK's prestigious military training academy Sandhurst. He also became a military pilot.

Sheikh Mo. is an accomplished athlete, but his real passion is horses

He wrote this about his favorite horse, 'Yezar.'

'Wide eyes tell you the horse is honest and loyal.

'Wide eyes tell you the greatness of a horse.

'A wide distance between ears means a big skull, a big brain. Brains don't mean fast; but it means the horse will understand you easily.

'Nose openings are a sign of endurance. Big openings mean the horse gets more oxygen; meaning larger lungs.

'Wide mout, means a wide oesophagus takes more air.

'The most important feature that helps judge a horse is the way they walk.

'Horses have a specific and special ratio that shapes the walk. And when you want to evaluate these proportions, the walk should be proportional.

'There was only one horse I owned that had all of the above.

'Yezar'

His personal international record in one equestrian event is phenomenal. It's called endurance riding: marathon running but with horses.

In 2012 he led the UAE team to a gold medal in an international tournament and he actually won the hundred and sixty-kilometer European Endurance Race in Italy.

That's Sheikh Mo's macho side covered.

He's also a prodigious writer of poetry and translated into dozens of languages.

He's very philanthropic and has donated billions of dollars to refugees in the Middle East. Closer to home he's known for visiting poorer areas of Dubai and surprising families by buying them villas.

He famously hates laziness and is feared for turning up in person unannounced at government buildings at seven thirty a.m. and firing any staff who were not at work on time, especially Emiratis.

For a leader of one of the wealthiest city-states on the planet he's remarkably accessible to locals.

It's said half of them have his cell-phone number on speed dial and if they can't get through it's open to any Emirati to visit his *diwan* - or receiving hall - when he's in town.

*Prison diary, September 14th 2013: Worried about cellmate Martin. He's gone cuckoo. New room-mate is Desi from Liberia caught smuggling gold.

*Prison diary, September 14th 2013: What I wouldn't pay for a whisky or a cold Stella.

The Sheikh's private life is less of an open book and long after I wrote my appeal to the Ruler's Court the wider world heard of alleged dark shenanigans behind palace walls.

Sheikh Mo has enthusiastically embraced polygamy; he is reported to have twenty-six wives; and to have fathered twenty-three children, give or take.

Most would have wished him good luck with that, until June 2019, when junior wife, Princess Haya Bint Al Hussein caused a sensation. She walked out on him, taking U.S.$50 million, telling tales of alleged cruelty and of wanting to start a new life.

Princess Haya, aged forty-five, and the younger half-sister of King Abdullah II of Jordan, is no shrinking violet.

She was schooled at Badminton in the UK and stayed in England to complete her A-level exams at exclusive Bryanston in Dorset. A brilliant scholar, she qualified to go up to Oxford, where she read Philosphy, Politics and Economics at St Hilda's College.

Like Sheikh Mo. she's a keen equestrian and in 2000 represented the Kingdom of Jordan at the Sydney Olympics in show jumping. Until 2019 the Princess was a familiar figure on the British horse racing circuit and was Vice President of the Royal Windsor Horse Show.

Soon after his wife deserted him Sheikh Mo. wrote poetry on his website, which appeared to lament her sudden disappearance.

'A fatal arrow has pierced my soul and left me insane,' the melancholy Sheikh wrote.

Then, he pleaded,

'Let the past be; soften your heart, forgive my mistakes, and reward my good deeds.'

Then: a complete U-turn. Suspecting she had a lover, he

posted a rant on Instagram accusing her of: *'betrayal,'* and added: *'Go, to whom you get busy with!!!!!?'*

Matters moved quickly and the couple's divorce case was listed for a first hearing at the end of July 2019 in London.

Sheikh Mo. hired barrister Helen Ward. She'd handled Guy Ritchie's split from Madonna, she also took on Formula 1 supremo Bernie Ecclestone's divorce from second wife Slavica, and pop singer Cheryl Cole, who was divorcing footballer Ashley Cole.

Princess Haya enlisted lawyer Fiona Shackleton, whose clients included Prince Charles in his divorce from Princess Diana and Prince Andrew in his split from the Duchess of York.

It wasn't the first time Sheikh Mo's turbulent family life caught headline writers' attentions.

Princess Haya's vanishing act was a disturbing postscript to two earlier episodes of apparent domestic turmoil in the Al-Maktoum household.

In 2018 an incredible story emerged that one of the Sheikh's daughters: Sheikha Latifa bint Mohammed Al Maktoum fled the family home claiming she'd been imprisoned and tortured.

Frenchman Hervé Jaubert, aged sixty two, who tried to help the princess escape, said he last spoke to her when he claimed he saw her being dragged off his vessel by the Indian coast guard screaming for political asylum.

Recounting the escape, he said his U.S.-flagged yacht was in international waters and off the coast of India when he noticed they were being tailed by the Indian coastguard. He claimed the 4th March 2018 incident was a full-blown military attack involving three boats and a surveillance plane. He claimed he was beaten up by the Indian authorities.

The Emirati princess has since been confirmed as being back home, but she has only been seen once when she appeared in photographs taken in Dubai during a visit by Mary Robinson, former president of Ireland and U.N. High Commissioner for Human Rights.

The highly publicised and bizarre meeting was panned by human rights groups for being stage-managed by the Emirati ruling family. Ms. Robinson is a 'personal friend' of the family.

Meanwhile campaigners like Human Rights Watch and Amnesty International have repeatedly asked for access to the Princess, but no requests have ever been answered.

In a statement the UAE government declared Latifa was, '*safe in Dubai*' and, '*looking forward to building a happy and stable future.*'

Sheika Latifa was the second of Sheikh Mo's daughters to allegedly disappear.

Latifa's older sister, Shamsa, was reportedly seized on the streets of Cambridge in the UK after fleeing the family's Surrey estate in 2000 and has not been seen or heard from since.

The allegation of kidnap was passed to David Beck, then a detective chief inspector in charge of Cambridge C.I.D. who told the BBC: 'Kidnap is a major offense and it's not every day that an allegation involving a head of state lands on a police officer's desk.'

But Beck couldn't take the investigation further. He needed to speak to Shamsa, but when he applied to visit Dubai to do so, the case hit a wall.

'*A short while later, I was informed that my request had been declined,*' he said. '*I was never given a reason why.*'

It's believed Shamsa spent eight years in prison on the orders of her father. Her disappearance and treatment were thought to have been a key factor in Princess Haya's decision to flee to London and seek a divorce.

Prison diary, September 20th 2013: I heard from Susan that Olivia was pinched by a boy at school. I, wished, I was home to guide her through what to do.

Prison diary, September 21s 2013: The lights have been fixed in our cell. Hurrah! I can read again.

So, there we had it. I was writing to a man whose word was the law in Dubai, a demi-god in his glamorous own world, a man who'd slept in a bed of scorpions, a friend of British royalty, a talented sportsman, game hunter and philanthropist.

Armed with his background I set out a brief history of my case and ended my application to the Ruler's Court like this:

'Since my arrest I have made more than 300 court appearances on criminal and civil charges

I have been cleared of all cases of fraud, as the court found no evidence of guilty intent.

But issuing a check without funds to cover it is an absolute criminal offense in Dubai carrying a sentence of up to three years on each charge. The courts have treated each case separately and given me consecutive sentences on each dishonored investors' check; thus, the reason for a forty-two-year sentence.

I am appealing to you your Highness, to please consider my case for clemency, I have never broken the law before, and my family are suffering.

I am in jail through no fault of my own. My company went bankrupt because of a fraudster, who himself is serving less of a sentence than I am, and he deliberately broke the law.

I could have left Dubai when my company collapsed at the end of 2008, but I stayed to try to compensate investors and do the honorable thing.

In my view a sentence of more than 40 years is disproportionately high. I would argue my criminal offense is, surely, single, relating to the issue of a series of checks that which were dishonored.

I have served almost four years now and would respectfully suggest this period is long enough for any wrongdoing. Being jailed has had a profound mental effect on me. I'm middle-aged, and I am effectively facing the possibility of spending the rest of my life in jail.

While staff at the jail have been kind and considerate, always, I desperately want to be with my daughter and my wife. Susan, my wife is finding it very difficult to cope as a lone parent; she is suffering from bouts of depression and at times finds it difficult to cope by herself. Our daughter Olivia is constantly asking where I am and when I am coming home. Olivia is growing up without a father as a role model to love and protect her and teach in a way that only a father can. My own father passed away recently which has completely left me devastated, I feel totally helpless.

I am deeply sorry that this has happened. I have apologised, unreservedly, to those involved, there was never an any ill intent, at any time, to defraud those concerned.

I have tried everything to reimburse those who invested their money, but they have requested that they receive their money plus the profits on property that was never built.

I genuinely love Dubai, my family and I were very happy

here and have very fond memories of our time here, before this happened. I would enjoy nothing more than to be released and continue to live Dubai again as a normal citizen in your country.

I respectfully request mercy and my freedom.
PETER MARGETTS.
DUBAI CENTRAL JAIL

14

Friends in high places

Prison diary, December 20th 2013: British guy tells me he was punched, Tasered, beaten and raped. The worst of this abuse was carried out by the prison guards and police.

Prison diary, December 21st 2013: Judge asked me if I was guilty in the fraud case. I said: 'no.' He adjourned the case and sent me back to jail; Hey ho!

In earlier chapters I described how my company went bust and the syndicate of Emirates pilots lost their massive investments, but I only told you half the story.

It wasn't just the collapse of the Dubai economy that brought the house of cards crashing down.

My firm had also fallen victim to an Iranian fraudster Hassan Sadri and I tell you his story now as salutary warning to any Western businessman operating in the Gulf: beware of Persian rip-off merchants operating from swanky offices.

I first met Sadri in early 2008 after my business partner Kieran answered a newspaper advertisement from a construction company looking for investors.

Kieran and I toddled along to the company Negar Estate

Holdings, which had an office in Bur Dubai, close to the Marco Polo hotel.

From first impressions Negar seemed respectable enough occupying an executive suite in a typical Dubai high-rise block. Beyond the office reception were mockups of various impressive construction projects.

Kieran and me were ushered into a room, where around twenty Afghan businessmen were gathered around the table along with Hassan Sadri, an unassuming man in his fifties, with grey hair and wearing dark trousers and, unusually for Dubai: a thick tweed jacket.

One of his assistants told us he was the company's CEO, but he spoke little English.

To be frank, I didn't feel comfortable with the Afghan audience. I'd no idea who they were and strangely none of them batted an eyelid when I asked them to leave the room. They simply upped and left on my command.

Then it was down to business. Through an interpreter, Sadri said he had two projects for sale. One, was a block of a hundred and twenty-five apartment units and the other: seventy-five units, both in up-market Jumeirah.

Sadri confirmed one hundred percent he owned the land and estimated construction would finish in eighteen months.

Hindsight is a wonderful thing, but before you judge me for making a rash decision can I remind you: at the time of our meeting in early 2008, the Dubai property market was still booming and fortunes were being made overnight for anyone wanting to dip a toe in the water.

Back then, you could buy an apartment for U.S.$500,000 in March and then flip it in April for at least U.S.$600,000 or even much more; easy money.

Looking back I should have known the property bubble would burst because there were rumblings in far off Wall Street of a possible financial crash, but even then, because Dubai was such a construction Klondike, bolstered by oil revenues and run by sheikhs as rich as Croesus, everyone, including me, believed the Emirates' property market was safe from collapse.

To cut a long story short, it was against this buoyant backdrop, and the potential of making as shed load of money, Kieran and I looked at Sadri's deal and thought we should go for it.

Sadri wanted a deposit of U.S.$4 million, which I thought was reasonable. I shook hands and wrote him four checks totaling that amount, firmly believing in eighteen months I'd be able to sell the land and apartments for a profit of around U.S.$7 million.

Kieran and I left Sadri's office walking on air. I really believed my fledgling company Hampstead and Mayfair was about to hit the big time. In that buoyant market I'd no qualms about signing other contracts for a fabulous set of apartments on a prestigious development at Dubai's Waterfront, which is where the ill-fated Emirates' pilots syndicate entered the picture.

So I could build at the Waterfront the pilots loaned me U.S.$7 million as investors. The lowest single amount each of the pilots chipped in was: U.S.$50,000; the highest: U.S.$500,000.

This amount was put in an escrow account and I confidently handed the syndicate of forty-two pilots post-dated security checks signed by me as Hampstead and Highgate CEO for the value of their loan to me, plus a guaranteed one-third profit.

I couldn't have been happier. That kind of big-time,

wheeler-dealering, was what I dreamt of when I first moved to the Far East, having put my wasted years behind me.

To add to my general feeling of joy my wife, Susan, and I were loving Dubai. We had a beautiful home and enjoyed a wonderful lifestyle: more, or less permanent sunshine, world-beating shopping malls, amazing sports facilities and a terrific social life.

Topping all of that: we'd recently been blessed with a beautiful daughter, Olivia.

Susan and I were on top of the world.

But then one morning, in late March 2008, only a week or two after we'd signed the contract with Hassan Sadri, came the first signs of trouble.

Kieran and I started to ask Sadri for paperwork, like: title documents and copies of various building licenses.

The charmer we met earlier suddenly became elusive and evasive. I wasn't unduly troubled. Time limits and deadlines, returning phone calls, were all a bit laissez-faire in that part of the world, so no need to worry too much, I thought.

But as months slid by Sadri stopped answering his phone and when we went to his office, we were told he'd left for the day.

When we couldn't get hold of him at all I started to panic. Without title, and other paperwork, I was screwed in terms of transferring the properties into my name.

So, I made an appointment at Dubai's RERA office, a government owned body I mentioned in an earlier chapter.

RERA's remit was to issue and regulate Dubai's maze of property laws, but also to hand out ownership certificates saying who owned which land and where. To my horror I discovered from RERA records Hassan Sadri wasn't the owner of the parcel of land at Jumeirah. It was someone else.

And that wasn't the end of it.

The final bombshell was when I discovered, through an associate, the bastard had cashed my deposit checks amounting to U.S.$4 million and done a runner to Iran.

Nobody I asked had any idea of Sadri's whereabouts in Iran and even if I could have got a visa to go look for him, wandering around the Islamic Republic, unable to speak Farsi, would have been like looking for a needle in the proverbial haystack

I was numb. The bastard had robbed me blind and there was nothing I could do.

Fast forward four years; against all odds, I got sweet revenge.

Prison diary, January 6th 2014: Again, due in 4 different courts for 4 different cases all at the same time. No lawyer. The more I am here, I realised, I'll be inside a long time. What a head fuck.

Prison diary, January 9th 2014: I had a kick-about in the yard with Jonny (Dutchman, money laundering) Nice man.

When Sadri ripped me off for U.S.$4 million and fled to Iran in December 2008, I'd reported him to police.

He'd been charged with theft, tried in his absence in Dubai and a lenient judge had sentenced him to just three years.

Prosecuting lawyers also told me if he was ever stupid enough to return to Dubai, they'd throw his sorry ass in jail.

Naturally, I thought I'd never see him again. I mean, surely, he'd not be stupid enough to return to Dubai?

One morning I came back from the exercise yard, sweating like a dog, to my utter bewilderment who was in my cell, sitting on the top bunk looking forlorn in prison pyjamas?

It was Hassan Sadri, the scoundrel who'd ripped me off.

He'd aged a lot and gone greyer since I'd seen last him, four years before. But, it was him, definitely.

I just stood there open-mouthed.

Sadri looked down from his bunk briefly, but he didn't recognise me from our last meeting in his office in Bur Dubai.

'Remember me?' I said.

No response. He looked puzzled.

'I'm Peter Margetts, the man you stole U.S.$4million dollars from.'

Sadri's jaw dropped like a stone. I saw sheer panic in his eyes.

Horrified, he let out a pathetic, cry: 'Don't kill me! Don't kill me!' and, quick as a flash he grabbed his bag of possessions and shot out of the cell like the hounds of hell were on his tail.

I dashed after him, but he'd found sanctuary among a clutch of prison guards who'd then shepherded him into another cell to be among fellow Iranians. They knew I couldn't get at him in an Iranians-only zone.

A lot of extraordinary things had happened to me in Dubai Central but to be confronted with the man who'd been party to destroying my life and that of my family, was utterly soul crushing.

Although he tried to give me a wide berth in the days and weeks that followed; he never wandered around without Iranian protection; I bumped into the little rat most days in the canteen and exercise yard.

I confess I wanted to murder him and mulled ways to bump the bastard off. In my mind I'd already opted for strangulation.

But then I came to my senses and told myself: 'Peter if you kill Sadri you'll never get out of jail and may even get the death sentence.'

So, I simply had to accept his presence in the jail.

Even though the most I ever did was to glare and verbally abuse him he was forever running to guards, like a spoilt brat, claiming I'd threatened to kill him.

One day I was called to prison governor Lt. Colonel Al-Hakim's office.

Half-jokingly he said: 'Peter, Peter, Peter. What are you doing to this man?

'I beg you please don't kill him. I have enough problems in this jail without another murder.'

I assured Al-Hakim I'd go easy however I made sure I remained on Sadri's tail, so he'd never be able to forget, not for one minute, what he'd done to me and my family.

At this point in the story let me introduce German John Schneider-Merck, a portly, grey-haired old buffer in his mid-sixties

Schneider-Merck wasn't an inmate, but a volunteer prison visitor who kept an eye on the welfare of German prisoners like my cellmate Martin.

When he popped in one day, I opened up to him about fraudster Sadri and how he'd stolen U.S.$4 million from me,

'Don't worry, Peter. I'll sort this out. I'll get to the bottom of it,' he assured me. He reminded me of former U.S. Secretary of State Henry Kissinger ending the Vietnam war

I was sceptical, but the kindly, old German worked his magic and sure enough, a week or so later, I was summoned to a meeting in governor Lt. Colonel Al-Hakim's office, where Sadri was already seated looking very nervous alongside an extremely sinister looking member of the UAE's *mukhabarat* or secret police. Schneider-Merck had organized it all.

I kid you not, the secret policeman bore a passing resemblance to Adolf Hitler complete with greasy, black hair with side parting, even a Führer-style moustache. I guessed he was no stranger to the art of pinning electrodes to genitals and he probably had a thumbscrew in his *dishdasha* pocket.

Sadri's extra-judicial interrogation began without the use of 240 volts. The Führer observed like a professional poker player looking across the table.

'Did you steal Mr. Margetts's money?' questioned the governor.

'Yes,' muttered Sadri straight off, his bottom lip quivered.

Then the Führer leaned menacingly close to Sadri's face. The terrified man was already clutching the arms of his chair. His knuckles glowed white.

'Do you still have Mr. Margetts's money?' the Führer growled.

'No, I gave it all to a friend,' Sadri replied.

That statement I knew to be baloney, because I'd heard he'd bought some land in Isfahan, Iran, soon after he'd swindled me.

Hakim carried on: 'Sadri, I'm ordering you to return Mr. Peter's money to him. I know you can find it'

Sadri nodded as Hakim continued: 'And I'll tell you this: you've been given a sentence of three years, but I promise you: you'll never, I repeat never, leave my prison until you pay the money back. You can be sure of that.'

The blood left Sadri's face.

Interrogation over I thanked John Schneider-Merck, Lt. Colonel Al-Hakim and the Führer for their help and returned to my cell with a smile.

The threat of permanent imprisonment from the prison

boss and one of the feared secret police wasn't a conventional method of enforcing justice, at least by Western standards, but it was a praiseworthy example how they handed out rough justice in Dubai.

After his grilling in Al-Hakim's office I saw little of Sadri after that, although I hoped he suffered a lot of sleepless nights wondering how he was going to raise four million bucks.

As far as I know, he's still behind bars.

I'm still waiting for my money back.

Prison diary, January 2nd 2014: I'm in some Orwellian nightmare of utterly incompetent 'lawyers,' none of whom appear to have read a law book and appearing in front of judges who know even less. To call them judges is a joke.

Prison diary, January 8th 2014: Prisoner, a former director of Leeds United Football club, tells me the only way to describe being in prison in Dubai is hell. He says he's been held for 22 months and he'll never forget it – the stench, the dirt, the smell, the heat, and the lack of any information whatsoever.

Extraordinary, John's Schneider-Merck, is worth a few more words.

A philanthropist, he made a name for himself intervening to help Germans imprisoned in foreign jails. One of his famous cases came in 2000 when he won freedom for German Helmut Hofer, who'd been sentenced to ninety-nine lashes followed by execution by hanging for having sexual relations with a Muslim woman in Teheran, Iran.

I wondered why Schneider-Merck was able to drop into

Dubai Central whenever he pleased to keep a grandfatherly eye on all German prisoners and ensure they stayed out of trouble?

And why did he have such a close relationship with prison governor: Lt. Colonel Al-Hakim?

After a few inquiries and chatting at length to John I'd worked it out.

Old Dubai hands and Emiratis often talked fondly about the good old days when the Dubai was barely developed in the early 1970s; an era when expats like Schneider-Merck arrived to set up business and to make a living in a city rising from the desert; a time in Dubai's history when unbreakable personal ties were formed with the locals.

'When I first came to Dubai, I immediately realized this was a pioneer country,' he said fondly.

'Everything was being built up. They were still digging out Jebel Ali port.

'The currency, although officially the *dirham*, was still colloquially called the *rupee*.'

'At the border of Dubai and Abu Dhabi there were still manned border posts, not like now of course.'

'There were no street names back then and directions were based on the few landmarks, such as a KFC fast-food restaurant or a nearby clock tower.'

'To find places, people put up balloons and visitors drove around looking for them,' he recalled

In common with other businessmen from that era Schneider-Merck developed a close relationship with the current Dubai Ruler's father, the revered Sheikh Rashid: 'I've been here since the days when you could just show up at Sheikh Rashid's house for a meeting and they just let you in, no problem,' he said.

Long after the sheikh's death his relationship with the royal inner circle continued to the present, so when Schneider-Merck wanted to visit Dubai Central he could pretty much come and go as he pleased; no questions asked of an honored guest.

The old German's other notoriety in the UAE was his fondness for animals, and cats in particular.

Locals admired him hugely for feeding forty feral felines every night outside his home in Sharjah.

'If at 4 p.m. we are not out with the food, they start protesting. They are the best-fed cats in Sharjah,' he said with a smile.

But Schneider-Merck's real place in the history books was; wait for it: tracking down the most notorious Gestapo chief: Klaus Barbie, the so-called Butcher of Lyon. Before moving to Dubai, Schneider-Merck lived in Peru, South America and used to regularly pay social visits to a German friend. A suspicious man used to also hang around the friend's house. He called himself Klaus Altmann.

Schneider-Merck recalled one incident: 'Once, I was saying that Hitler had destroyed the reputation of Germany.'

'Then that man stood up in a rage and said: 'In my presence, no one will say anything negative about der Führer.'

After that outburst Schneider-Merck became suspicious, even more so when he looked at his ears! According to him: Barbie apparently had distinctively shaped ears.

'As you get older, many things change,' he said. 'But the ears, they stay the same,' he added eruditely.

To cut a long story short, Schneider-Merck contacted Nazi hunter Simon Wiesenthal and those early suspicions played a role in the eventual extradition of Barbie to France, where he was put on trial for war crimes and sentenced to life imprisonment. Barbie died in prison of leukemia just four years later aged seventy-seven.

Modestly understating his role in the capture of one of the world's most wanted fugitives Schneider-Merck said: 'Those were interesting times.'

After his role in Sadri's fate, I realised Schneider-Merck was a good guy to have on your side. I'm glad he'd been on mine!

Prison diary, January 28th 2014: It's the end of another shitty month. It's Desi's birthday. He said grace before our meals at my request. Not often asked for that and it felt good.

Prison diary, January 29th 2014: Brother-in-law Karsten arrives for a visit with son Nathan who says he has a new girlfriend.

My Member of Parliament in the UK, Zac Goldsmith had enthusiastically taken my case up with the Foreign and Commonwealth Office in London and an appeal for action by the government, particularly over my effective life sentence, had landed in the in-tray of Foreign Minister Alistair Burt. His initial response was not encouraging and not what I wanted to hear.

Burt wrote back to Goldsmith essentially repeating the British Embassy in Dubai's position. The minister said he, *'felt sorry,'* for my situation and he: *'appreciated the distress.'* being caused to my wife and child but: *'appropriate consular assistance was being given.'*

Crushing my hopes the UK government would fight for my release, Burt added that his government couldn't interfere in another country's legal system just as any other nation mustn't try to influence the UK's.

Burt's letter of reply then referred Zac to a human rights pressure group in London called Fair Trials International, founded in 1992 by lawyer Stephen Jakobi supported by the likes of Labour Party politician, Lord Falconer.

'Perhaps they can provide assistance,' said the minister ending his letter in a helpful tone.

Unfortunately, what Foreign Minister Burt didn't know, John Cookson had already visited FTI's office's in The Temple, London and urged them for help.

But my case didn't quite fit their profile, and their representative said so. They were quite open about that.

Indeed, the plight of a middle-aged, white, British businessman sitting in a Dubai jail, charged with bouncing checks, didn't excite the imaginations of any prominent human rights agencies and high-profile lawyers John contacted.

He'd written to Michael Mansfield QC, perhaps the most prominent of them all; famed for winning freedom for the so-called Birmingham Six. Mansfield never replied to John.

Zac Goldsmith persisted with the Foreign Office. John kept up the pressure and met with minister Alistair Burt in Basrah, Iraq, during a visit and urged him to investigate my case.

And five months after his first letter Burt wrote to Zac again.

To my utter surprise and relief Burt said he'd taken a personal interest in my story!

Not only that, he said he'd discussed my case with his UAE opposite number: Foreign Minister Anwar Mohammed Gargash in Abu Dhabi.

He also revealed British Consul General Guy Warrington had asked the Dubai Government why I was being charged with forty two checks offenses, resulting in me being sentenced to forty two years, when under Dubai law they ought to have been treated as one case with a maximum penalty of three years.

This was amazing news. At last, I thought, someone big was working on my side and that someone was none other than the British government! Fantastic!

And it got better. I'd already heard Downing Street had taken an interest and Zac; I will always be grateful for this; raised a question to the Foreign Office Minister Hugh Robertson in the House of Commons.

Here is an extract from the official record: Hansard.

'Zac Goldsmith: To ask the Secretary of State for Foreign and Commonwealth Affairs what recent consular support his Department has provided to Peter Margetts in Dubai Central Jail. [169937]

Hugh Robertson: Consular officials, both at the Foreign and Commonwealth Office in London and at the British embassy in Dubai, have been providing Mr. Margetts with consular assistance since his initial detention.

Mr. Margetts' welfare continues to be our main priority and I would like to reassure you that consular officials continue to monitor his case closely and will follow up on any welfare concerns.

Consular officials most recently spoke to Mr. Margetts on 8 October. During this call Mr. Margetts informed consular officials that he did not need a visit and that he would call when he needed assistance. He also requested that consular officials send a message to your office, which they have subsequently done.

Zac Goldsmith: To ask the Secretary of State for Foreign and Commonwealth Affairs what recent representations he has made to the Government of the United Arab Emirates on the hunger strike of Peter Margetts in Dubai Central Jail. [169938]

Hugh Robertson: Consular officials, both at the Foreign and Commonwealth Office in London and at the British embassy in Dubai, have discussed the hunger strike at regular points with the prison authorities. More widely, consular officials continue to monitor his case closely and will follow up on any welfare concerns.

Consular officials most recently spoke to Mr. Margetts on 9 October. He has also requested that consular officials update your office, which they have subsequently done.

14 Oct 2013: Column 549W'

On hearing my case had been raised in the House of Commons - for fuck's sake! - I felt the end was in sight.

Surely, I thought, all this coverage would have some impact on, the Dubai Government, and they'd let Peter Margetts walk free?

15

Sex on the beach

*Prison diary, September 8th 2015: I need a change of cell. Trouble is you have long termers like me and Martin and those who only got 1 year and who have different values and agenda. It used to stress me when they talked about their short sentences.

*Prison diary, September 10th 2015: I slept all day which was unusual. It was cold because of the cell air-con was on high. I was feeling very low. I'd been robbed of a few things. I'd be killed if I complained.

Waiting for news of my appeal to the Ruler's Court and a breakthrough in talks between the UAE and UK governments lasted through 2015 and into 2016. To say it was a glacial pace, hardly sums things up!

I could have benefitted from some publicity to help my cause, but journalists who'd given the hunger strike tons of publicity, had lost interest because frankly there was nothing concrete to write about me; nothing new to spark a news editor's interest.

Not that Brits falling foul of Dubai's laws weren't providing the UK tabloids with masses of stories the whole time I was in jail, not least the so-called sex-on-the-beach cases which to that seemed to crop up every month or so.

At the time of my arrest Dubai police had nabbed a Lebanese woman and her female Bulgarian lover making out on a beach at Manzar Park.

A witness described the torrid scene to police: 'The Lebanese woman was lying on top of the Bulgarian, they were kissing and cuddling each other in front of us.'

The pair got a month's jail each and then deported.

A week or so later another other sensational case had the British press slobbering.

Vince Acors, who was thirty four, had been on a five-day business trip to Dubai when he was arrested for, let's say: cavorting with fellow Brit Michelle Palmer, who was two-years older. Earlier the pair had hooked up at an all-you-can-drink champagne bash at the Le Meridien hotel.

Acors told the Sunday Mirror newspaper: *'I found myself on a warm beach with a not unattractive woman. We were both drunk and we went for it!'*

Acors added: *'I just laid back and thought of Bromley!'* (a South London suburb.)

In court their lawyers claimed no actual intercourse had taken place. Both were jailed briefly and then deported but not before, according to friends, they underwent a form of wedding ceremony to keep the judge happy!

On his release Acors said: *'Yes, we did wrong but neither of us could ever have dreamed that five-minutes of slap and tickle would get us thrown in jail!'*

It wasn't only slap and tickle that got the authorities in Dubai in a funk. Officially, drugs were an absolute no-no, although if you were an Emirati and got caught the courts would usually go easy as they did with other crimes locals committed.

Britons Keith Brown and his wife were flying from London to Ethiopia and were stopped and searched at Dubai Airport as part of a routine check. Customs officers spotted a roll-up cigarette in the tread of Mr. Brown's shoe, not even a proper cigarette.

Astonishingly, forty-three-year-old Mr. Brown, was charged with the possession of a minuscule piece of cannabis, in size less than a grain of sugar, and sentenced to four years. After a public outcry back in the UK he was released early.

Then, there was the case of a BBC Radio One Disc jockey called 'Grooverider.' He was jailed for having a speck of marijuana in his jeans pocket at Dubai airport. His lawyer argued in court his client had no intention of bringing the drug into Dubai and had forgotten he'd recently been in contact with hash.

'Grooverider' served ten months.

Then there were other so-called obscene acts which in Dubai included: swearing aloud, making rude gestures, slandering someone on social media, even an angry text.

A British woman faced two years in jail for calling her ex-husband's new wife: 'a horse,' on Facebook. Fifty-five-year old, Laleh Shahravesh, was arrested at a Dubai airport after flying there to attend her former husband's funeral. Ms. Shahravesh's fourteen-year-old daughter, Paris, wrote to Dubai's Ruler Sheikh Mohammed asking for her mother's release. The British Foreign office also intervened, and she was eventually freed.

Twenty-seven-year old Jamie Harron's case made headlines for a while in the UK.

He was a tourist from Scotland who accidentally brushed past a stranger in a bar in Barsha Heights.

Harron, was accused of drunkenly touching a Jordanian businessman and, following his trial, he was jailed for three months. A tabloid and 'twitter storm' erupted and Sheikh Mo. intervened again. He quashed the conviction.

Prison diary, March 8th 2014: Susan asked me if I would ever get out. It upset me she thought there was little or no hope.

Prison diary, March 9th 2014: Lunch was Pot Noodle. No sandwiches. Needed to get my brain working again.

Having read about this frippery we inmates chatted amongst ourselves and our eyes rolled to be honest. There we were doing hard-core jail-time and battling to get our over-lengthy sentences reduced; however, the UK newspapers didn't want to know about us. We assumed there was nothing titillating about our stories.

As we sat in our cells chewing over each tawdry case, we agreed the fact they'd even come to court had highlighted Dubai's shocking hypocrisy and double standards.

Let me explain, whilst the authorities were busy prosecuting wayward Brits for slap and tickle, the city-state had already become notorious as one of the world's money laundering capitals, a crossroads for the illegal arms trade and, a center for prostitution on an industrial scale.

The man dubbed the world's biggest money launderer, Naresh Kumar Jain, an Indian multi-millionaire ran his empire out of Dubai shifting U.S.$1.5 billion a year before he was arrested in Delhi by India's 'narco' cops.

Jain admitted he laundered money through Dubai, but denied he was in the drugs trade.

Meanwhile drug money linked to the Afghan heroin trade was washed through Dubai, to bank-roll the Taliban militant group trying to topple the regime in Kabul. The 9/11 bombers were financed though Dubai's banking system by Al Qaeda.

Arms smuggling was another of the UAE's open secrets. African dictators and rebels like Liberia's Charles Taylor used Dubai and Sharjah as a supply base for illegal weapons.

And when rogue Pakistani scientist, A. Q. Khan, was selling his country's nuclear technology to states like Iran and Libya, he used Dubai as a black market for parts for an atom bomb. Centrifuges, special tubing, lathes all passed through Dubai's free port unhindered. Khan also made multiple visits to Dubai until he was shut down in 2004. He even underwent a vasectomy there.

On a more mundane level, dozens of high-speed vessels skim across the Strait of Hormuz back and forth from Dubai after dark to the Iranian coast with illicit goods like gold, whisky and arms. They often bring heroin back.

And each evening, *dhows* with hidden cargoes of smuggled gold set off from Dubai Creek bound for the Pakistan, Indian, Sri Lankan coast for a rendezvous at sea with Asian mobsters who exchange it for cash, drugs and arms for the return journey.

The world's mafia organizations freely use Dubai as a bolt-hole.

Even as I wrote this book, Irish media reported a Dublin-based mob boss was living it large in Dubai hobnobbing with Italy's most feared mafia dons; members of the Ndrangheta gang from Calabria, suspected of supplying Europe with half its cocaine.

So, make no mistake: dirty money is integral to modern Dubai's foundations. Terror groups, organised crime and drug cartels, have cleaned billions of dollars there, and still do.

As for prostitution, religiously straightlaced Dubai is also awash with whorehouses. I could take you to several four, and five star, hotels, members of international chains, where hookers, mostly from Eastern Europe or North Africa, openly ply their trade in bars, lobbies and around swimming pools. More than once I've been accosted in a hotel elevator.

Such is Dubai's apparent openness to prostitution. I remember a time in the mid-2000s when sex-workers, flying in from Russia and Eastern Europe, effectively had their own special line at passport control at Dubai International.

Soliciting is illegal, of course, but crime syndicates including the Russian mafia, have cornered the Dubai market paying off lowly-paid doormen and security guards to allow the girls access to hotels. The girls also include ladyboys from the Far East whom I mentioned in a previous chapter.

Demand for girls, is huge.

It's partly the way Dubai markets itself, as a sun-soaked playground, a glamorous, alcohol-fuelled, bastion of hedonism, where anything goes, as long as it's behind closed doors.

'A paradise of pork, prostitutes and pina coladas,' is how one writer described it.

Prostitution also thrives, because Dubai is, essentially, a city of men. Women make up only a quarter of the population and fourteen percent of the workforce.

Ninety-five percent of Dubai's residents are foreign workers and expat employees are mostly male working in ministries, private corporations, hospitals and similar institutions.

Dubai's also home to hundreds of thousands of young and frisky Muslim bachelors from the Indian sub-continent and Far East. They've never had easy access to women, often due to social and religious constraints, meaning they're like kids in a candy store once they land in Dubai.

Of course, the Dubai government is aware of all of the above: the money laundering, arms dealing and prostitution rackets but either turns a blind-eye or tolerates it for expedience.

For my cellmates and I, what used to really stick in our craws was that, Ruler Sheikh Mohammed routinely put out statements to the media like: *'In Dubai there will be no tolerance shown to anybody who tries to exploit his position to make illegal profits.'*

What hypocrisy.

Prison diary, May 10th 2014: Realising I needed to control my temper more. I fly off the handle easily.

Prison diary, May 11th 2014: Bully thought he was being released. But they kept him. Another week and he'll flip out.

Tolerance of organised crime, or deliberately ignoring it, doesn't explain why the Ruler's men prosecuted the small fry, the so-called sex-on-the-beach cases, which triggered so much bad publicity for Dubai in the Western media.

I had plenty of time, in jail, to mull over this anomaly too.

First, you needed to examine Dubai's headlong push for expansion and the wealth and social change that it's brought for ordinary Emiratis

Sheikh Mohammed's rule, so far, has seen the construction of at least five-hundred luxury hotels, world beating shopping malls, and apartment blocks spread across an area the size of Manhattan.

During my years in jail the tourism industry alone was worth around U.S.$23 billion a year.

It's brought an unimaginable windfall for Emiratis, of whom there are only 100,000 in a city of 2 million.

Their newfound wealth also includes billions of dollars from the oil and gas industry.

As well as living an easy life in a world-class city, every Emirati male receives a U.S.$50,000 subsidy a year and U.S.$19,000 toward his wedding costs. Health care is free, so is education, food and gas for vehicles is subsidized. There's no income or property tax and Emirati teens get free access to universities in Europe and the U.S.

Citizenship is jealously guarded. Even if an Emirati woman marries, say: a Kuwaiti man, neither he, nor their children, can obtain citizenship.

Fewer than ten percent of UAE nationals are employees in a conventional job, so in short Emiratis are some of the wealthiest, most pampered citizens on Earth.

However, as we've seen, for all its apparently freewheeling ways, Dubai is not the liberal, hedonistic playground advertised by its tourism industry.

In exchange for their enviable wealth, Emiratis are prepared to turn a blind eye to organised crime, and money laundering, but only to a point.

What infuriates conservative, highly religious families is what they see as Western immorality, paraded in public. They fear it may corrupt their own youth.

From time to time, moral outrage boils over in the Arabic press and on local radio phone-ins and unelected Sheikh Mohammed, who keeps his ear to the ground, is intelligent enough to realise he and his extended family are only there at the whim of the people, so he needs to keep them happy, in a land of strong tribal loyalties.

As a result, from time to time, there's a crackdown on Western excesses and that's why sex-on-the-beach performers Mr. Acors, and his girlfriend, found themselves arrested and taken into custody.

I need to re-emphasise something here: Me, and other respectable businessmen in jail with me, weren't behind bars because some head of a Dubai family was sounding off about a decline in moral values.

None of us had sex on the beach. We weren't money launderers, terrorists or mafia dons. We weren't killers who'd served our time, but didn't have enough to pay so-called blood money

Our offenses arose, from the collapse of the Dubai economy, plus an unjust checks law, which had sent me and others tumbling headlong into a chaotic pastiche of a justice system devoid of humanity and decency, presided over by incompetent clowns.

16

The Pink Panthers

Prison diary, December 20th 2016: Dave punched me. Earlier, he'd been released, but sent back when they found another case against him. He got another month. He's psychotic, definitely.

Prison diary, December 25th 2016 Christmas dinner arrived. A Pot Noodle, a Snickers bar and a Pepsi. Please God: let me be free, let me see my family, let me breath fresh air, let me kiss my wife, let me visit my dad's grave. I'm still in the game - never surrender!

While the months rolled by, there was nothing I could do, but try to stay safe, make the best of it, soak up the experience and hopefully leave jail a stronger person. Peter Margetts is ever the optimist!

As you've heard, there was no shortage of characters to try to rub along with, both inmates and jail visitors.

Dubai Central was a real melting pot for the famous, and infamous! Maradona's visit for example, Nazi hunter Schneider-Merck and others. Well, let me introduce you to the Pink Panther gang.

In 2007 Dubai witnessed a stunning jewellery heist. A four-man gang stole two Audi cars, one black, the other white and smashed through the front gates of Al-Wafi mall, scattering terrified shoppers. Then, they crashed spectacularly into their target: The House of Graff, jewellery store.

Like a scene from a Hollywood thriller, the gang, with faces covered by masks and dressed in black, stormed into the Graff store wielding hammers and replica firearms

After smashing glass display cabinets, they fled with swag-bags bulging with precious jewels and watches worth around U.S.$13.5 million.

Amazingly, the whole operation had taken only seconds and even police conceded the raid had been perfectly executed by professionals who'd burned their getaway cars in nearby Za'abeel Road, wiping out evidence.

But, who were these professionals, famed for executing Dubai's biggest robbery?

It came as no surprise when police revealed they were looking for the members of the notorious Pink Panther gang, so-called because, in a previous heist, they'd stolen a massive jewel by pressing it into a jar of face cream, copying a tactic in the movie The Return of the Pink Panther, starring Peter Sellers.

Before the Dubai job, the Pink Panthers already had a formidable reputation and growing following amongst the criminal fraternity, having been credited with ninety spectacular robberies in Europe, the United States and the Far East, including Japan.

And it wasn't the first time they'd struck Graff. Four years before two gang members had stolen U.S.$23 million worth of jewellery from the company's store in London's Sloane Street.

By 2007, the Pink Panther gang, had netted a quarter of a billion US dollars in stolen loot, making them the world's most wanted robbers with a matchless reputation.

After a heist in France, a judge in Chambery said: 'We're dealing with hardened, professional delinquents. Most of them are very intelligent. The artistry of the criminals can be seen in their attention to detail and impeccably planned heists.'

Interpol, the international police force, revealed Pink Panther gang members were mostly former special forces officers from armies in the former Yugoslavia, nationals of countries like Serbia, Bosnia and Croatia. Apparently, they were able to change their identities and passports and spoke several languages, effortlessly.

They hardly ever got caught. Except when the Dubai police got lucky!

They recovered most of the stolen jewels from the Graff heist, after they intercepted a car with the gems stashed in the panelling.

Police made, a number of arrests, including Borko Ilincic and Nicola Milat, who were convicted of the Dubai robbery and were inmates in Dubai Central.

Nicola was a terrific guy. He was very fit, and a keen sportsman, in his early thirties. I often played football with him and we had long conversations in the exercise yard.

All cons maintain they are innocent, but I believed Nicola.

He insisted he'd had nothing to do with the Graff robbery and burst out laughing at the suggestion he was a member of the Pink Panther gang.

The reason why I thought he was telling the truth was because he told me police had held him in solitary for ten days, they'd tortured him and forced him to sign a confession in Arabic, a language he neither spoke nor understood.

I didn't press him on how a confession had been forced out of him, but it was a familiar story. Having heard similar accounts from other inmates it normally meant he'd been beaten and had an electric prodder used on his body.

In court, Nicola had been found guilty of aiding and abetting the Dubai robbery and initially handed a ten-year sentence, increased to twenty years on appeal.

'Peter, I have absolutely no idea why I was arrested,' he told me one day.

'The only thing I can think of is, I run a business in Dubai and I went to Belgrade on holiday and met a girl in a bar and she asked me how Serbs got visas for Dubai, as the two countries don't have diplomatic relations. I told her how to use company who specialised in visas.'

'Maybe, she was a member of the Pink Panther gang, or an associate? That's all I can think of.'

I wasn't the only one with doubts about Nicola's conviction. His persistent family, persuaded the UN to intervene and a report by the UN Commission on Arbitrary Detention, dated 31st August 2010, criticized the Dubai authorities and noted: *'the only evidence against Milat was his written statement in Arabic, which he signed while in detention without an interpreter and a lawyer. None of the 18 witnesses heard during the trial linked Milat to the robbers.'*

I'm pleased to report Nicola was deported home to Serbia in 2013.

The other man convicted of the Dubai Graff robbery in jail with me was a very different case.

After the Graff heist, Serb national, Borko Ilincic, had been arrested in Spain, traveling on a forged Bosnian passport.

He was extradited to the UAE and initially given ten years, but prosecutors demanded a life term after he lodged an appeal.

He never mixed with us on a social basis; a bit of a loner; although I often saw him in the exercise yard. His heavily tattooed body was muscular, he was aged about thirty-three, with short, black hair, his face was boyish and always with a week's worth of stubble.

And, like many prisoners from the Balkans, he was the archetypal hard bastard, best given a wide berth.

One morning, we heard Ilincic been found hanged in his cell. A report said he'd used his own clothing.

His was just the latest in a series of puzzling suicides in Dubai Central, and we inmates kept an open mind on how he died.

17

Blood money

Diary, January 3rd 2017: A judge tells me he wants to see all my files which is encouraging. is this the beginning of the end?

Diary, January 5th 2017: My pro-bono British barrister forwarded photos of my family. He'll never know what that means to someone locked-up. It's such a boost to the soul.

Although the plight of check case prisoners like me was horrendous, there was one group of inmates in Dubai Central for whom I felt especially sorry.

They were the two dozen or so prisoners, who'd served their time, but hadn't been released, because they couldn't afford to pay so-called 'blood money' to their victims' families.

Blood money, or *diya* in Arabic, is an automatic U.S.$55,000 payable for killing someone in, say, a road accident.

Diya could be a lot more if the accident victim survived and suffered multiple injuries. U.S.$25,000 was the price for a lost limb and there were additional amounts for brain damage and general pain; put bluntly: it was often cheaper for the perpetrator who caused an accident to kill someone than to maim them.

Pakistani bus driver Humayun Al Rahman was in jail

with me.

He'd been driving migrant workers from their labor camp in Jebel Ali to their workplace in Al Waraqaa when he lost control of his bus and slammed into a minibus. Ten people died in the carnage.

He was sentenced to three years in jail and eventually received a pardon.

But, he was also ordered to pay, U.S.$500,000 in blood money before he could be released, an impossible sum for a bus driver earning 300 bucks a month!

Another Pakistani in jail with me caused a fatal road crash that killed two people. He finished his sentence in 2009, but he was still behind bars because there was no way he could pay $US110,000 in blood money.

In all these cases, lawyers argued their clients had no chance of a release date because they were caught in a catch 22.

To pay blood money they needed a job. They couldn't get a job because they were in jail. So how the heck were they going to pay off their debt?

The blood money payments system is changing with charities working with the government to help prisoners like driver Al-Rahman pay off what they owe. There's also a move to force insurance companies to pick up the bill.

But to this day the blood money system is still very much in play in Dubai with around U.S.$8million paid to victims' families every year.

Those who can't pay remain in jail even though they've served their sentence.

18

Me versus the Emirates pilots

Prison diary, May 1st 2017: An Iranian guy called me:' Peter the cheater.' Sorely tempted to belt him. Some people revel in others' misery. He crossed the line

Prison diary, May 2nd 2017: We were woken in the early hours, someone had escaped. These are getting regular. Our pet, Kevin, the Kitten also missing. Perhaps he's fucked off too. Can't blame him.

I returned from court one evening, after another wasted day in the hands of Dubai's useless legal system to find a crisp, white envelope with my name typed on the front on my bunk. Whoever sent it must have bribed prison bosses because letters weren't allowed to be left for inmates in their cells.

Inside I found a note from one of my clients: an Emirates' pilot, writing on behalf of himself and others in the syndicate.

The stark, one-line message read: *'Pay us back, then you can go home.'*

At first, I just gazed at it, mesmerised, for a few moments. Then, I felt my stomach tightening.

How could I begin to return the pilots' money? I was behind bars and both myself and my company were bankrupt. To raise money, I needed to be free, go meet contacts, bankers, put together payments plan. None of this was possible while I was behind bars in Dubai Central.

As I mentioned in previous chapters, I understood the pilots' fury. They'd lost a lot of money, life savings in some cases. The smallest individual losses were around U.S.$50,000; the most: about U.S.$500,000 in the ill-fated property deal at the heart of this story which also left my business in ruins and me, the fall-guy, in jail.

As the months and years dragged by since that original note the pilots had hired a top Dubai law firm: Al Tamimi -350 lawyers, seventeen offices in the Middle East - which to that had close ties to the ruling family.

As lawyers do when they spy helpless prey: they put a boa constrictor squeeze on me by not only taking out what's known as Mareva injunction, which froze any assets I had anywhere in the world including my home in Richmond, London, and they brought a prosecution against me for fraud.

The injunction I felt I could handle and even as this book is written my UK lawyer is trying to get it lifted.

But, the allegation of fraud was the real killer. A serious, 'white-collar', crime, it carried a heavy sentence in Dubai, to add to my forty two years, and more importantly: I, Peter Margetts, may have been a lot of things, but I was not a fraudster.

True, I'd been involved in the collapse of a business deal in which the pilots lost a lot of money, but the cause of that was not my incompetence. It was brought about by the collapse of the Dubai economy. I'd lost millions too, as well as landing in jail.

So, right at the start of the fraud proceedings I admitted I'd signed checks, which bounced; however, I vehemently rejected the accusation I'd committed an act of fraud against the pilots.

The fraud case had dragged on at least two years when two days before the final hearing I had a visit in jail from another Emirates pilot: Peter Krygger, a square-jawed, no-nonsense Aussie in his fifties; Krygger, was still smarting because he'd lost U.S.$500,000 in the failed deal. I would have been fit-to-be-tied if I were he. I felt very sorry for him.

By then he'd become the self-appointed leader of the group of pilots.

He'd brought with him a couple of other pilots and a female lawyer from Al Tamimi who demanded to see my bank statements and other evidence relating to accounts, which I no longer possessed or had access to.

We ran over the various incarnations of a settlement plan I'd previously offered the pilots, involving raising money to buy another plot of land for construction. They were having none of it.

I felt ambushed. I reminded them it was inappropriate for accusers to pay a visit to a defendant without his lawyer present whilst a fraud trial was on going and two days before the verdict.

Long story short: I sent them packing.

On the final day of the fraud hearing I heard from a court clerk the judge was keen to deliver his verdict and to get away, as he had a holiday in Greece booked!

And there was massively good news for me. Even the court translator smiled: 'Mr. Margetts, you've been found not guilty of fraud.'

'You're free to go.'

What she meant of course: I was at liberty—but to go back to jail.

I whooped with joy and looked across the court at the devastated faces of Krygger and others.

That wasn't the end of it. They lodged an appeal. But that was also rejected. Only then did I feel I'd been finally been vindicated and had not committed fraud.

I met one more time with Krygger. He said: 'Look, Peter, I don't want you to think this was personal.'

I couldn't believe what he'd just said about the pursuit of me not being personal

Had one of the pilots not presented their post-dated security check for payment there would have been no prosecution of me, and, I still believed I could have pulled together a rescue package, had I not been in jail.

Not personal, when my life had been destroyed? And not only mine but my wife and my daughter's.

There was one other matter Krygger raised at the end of our last conversation.

'Now then Peter, why don't you pay mine and the other pilots' legal fees. They're about two million *dirhams* (U.S.$500,000),' he said in the tone pilots use when they wish you a pleasant onward journey.

My immediate thought: he was having a laugh, so I responded: 'No, sorry, won't be doing that. No can do.'

However, after he left, I wondered: had he heard something about my bid to win freedom, either personally or through Al Tamimi, the law firm with close ties with the ruling family?

Could the unthinkable be happening? Was Krygger making one last bid to salvage something from the wreckage, before they let me go?

I didn't have to wait long for the answer.

19

False start

Prison diary, May 15th 2017: The communal phone cut off again. It did that when anyone swore down the line. I'd dropped the 'f 'bomb that's why.

Prison diary, May 18th 2017: Had a dream about a meal in Pizza Hut. Woke in the early hours and heard two Emiratis having sex in a cell down the corridor. One was squealing!

Looking back, it was probably at the start of the Muslim holy month of Ramadan in May 2017 when I first dared to believe I might be released early, after more than eight long years behind bars.

Maybe that's too strong. Let's say: the smoke signals I picked up hinted something, just something, might be in the works. Perhaps you could say my sense of optimism helped make two and two add up to four.

As I mentioned in the previous chapter, Emirates' pilot Peter Krygger seemed desperate at our last meeting to get some money out of me, so had he heard they were planning to let me go?

Plus, it was Ramadan, normally a time when the Ruler,

Sheikh Mohammed, emphasised his ties with deity by granting clemency for hundreds of prisoners. Rumors swept the jail, check cases like me could be first in line for the exit.

But it was all froth, based on no factual evidence, just gossip among men who had little else to do all day. And, of course, the stories got bigger and better by the telling because we wanted to believe them.

What was not hot air were on-going efforts behind the scenes by my MP Zac Goldsmith to win my release and my own application for hearing at the Ruler's Court.

I'd heard no update, but I firmly believed pressure was beginning to build on the Dubai government to let me go.

I should mention I'd also filed papers for an early release for good behavior. I'd been a good guy, stayed out of trouble from the day I entered jail, so why not?

In fact, it was me chasing news on my early release application that prompted me to wander over to the prison office late one afternoon to find out if there'd been a response.

The office was in the usual state of organized confusion; phones ringing off the hook, prisoners queuing for bits of paperwork and fax machines churning out reams of sheets that stood a strong chance of never being read or simply buried in files.

I'd taken my place in the line when I eyed, through the forest of filing cabinets, a really good friend: a rotund, middle-aged Omani office clerk called Ali.

As soon as Ali saw me waiting in line he started beaming, then, he pointed a finger in my direction, made an arm gesture of a plane taking off and mouthed: whoosh!

After over eight years in jail you can understand my

scepticism at that point.

I thought: 'Fuck, does he mean what I think he means?'

Ali walked over: 'Peter, you're leaving. I've seen the paperwork.'

'It's going to happen.'

I didn't know how to respond. I'd seen no piece of paper saying I was being released and I knew in that part of the world, without a serious chitty, signed in triplicate, you were going nowhere, especially walking out of Dubai Central Jail.

I thanked Ali most sincerely, left him with his whirring fax machines and headed back to my cell; my head was spinning.

I was bursting with joy and wanted to tell the world, however I deliberately forced myself not to erupt into raptures. I was right not to say anything because two days passed and nothing.

On the third a guard walked into my cell mid-morning and said, quite off the cuff: 'You finish here. *Helas!* You leave.'

Then, he brusquely gestured me to get my possessions together.

From his forthright manner, I could see, I was definitely going somewhere. But where?

Some of the other lads, like Mark, Ryan and Charles were open-jawed, as they watched me grab my two plastic buckets all prisoners were given to keep personal effects in, which I started to fill.

Wherever I was going I knew the buckets were too small to hold all my stuff, so I began giving away the little extra luxuries I'd coveted and collected over the previous eight and a half years, like an extra pillow, a fistful of telephone cards and an MP3 player.

I can't remember now in what order I handed them to check case cellmates like Mohammed, a Libyan, Wael from

Egypt, and UK-born Rajumani, such was my excitement, and such was their joy!

A couple of young Colombian friends, Jose and Juan, both of whom were convicted burglars, also copped for some of my unwanted possessions as guards urged me to follow them with my two buckets, and swiftly finish my goodbyes.

On the way to the jail's reception I bumped into another good friend Faisal: a terrific French football player who in his glory days played for UK team Bristol City, but who was currently serving ten years for robbery: 'Hope to see you on the outside Peter,' he cried as I was hurried along.

I gave him a thumbs up.

In reception I was joined by five other prisoners, and we were handed possessions taken away from us on day one: credit cards, gym membership tags and suchlike.

They also returned my civilian clothes: a pair of shoes, grey track suit bottoms and a stinking, unwashed T-shirt which my wife Susan had brought to the jail years before and were now six sizes too big, because I'd lost so much weight.

As I struggled into them, I had to grip the track suit pants' waistband to stop them, falling down.

I said to myself under my breath: 'One step at a time Peter, they haven't returned your passport, so you can't be going far. Don't too excited.'

'Get on the bus,' the guards shouted.

'Where are we going,' I asked.

No answer.

'You've got to tell me where you're taking me.'

'We take you Al Rashidiya.'

'*Yellah,* let's go!'

'Al Rashdiya?' I gasped. 'Oh, my fucking God!'

Of course, Al Rashidiya, the notorious police hellhole, was where my nightmare began all those years ago. Surely, this was not happening?

As the bus trundled across desert scrubland leaving Dubai Central far behind my elation about possibly being released evaporated and I sank into a deep depression.

'They're not releasing you just transferring you to another facility,' I told myself.

In Dubai City Al Rashidiya eventually loomed like a bad dream. It felt like my horror story was starting over especially as I was shoved into a cell block with the others where we waited fifteen hours in handcuffs. The only saving grace was I wasn't back in the chamber I'd first been thrown into all those years before.

There was no food served during Ramadan during daylight hours, so I got nothing to eat from early morning until the following day when they handed out boxes of cooked rice and vegetables at three a.m.

By then I was utterly exhausted emotionally, with barely enough energy to eat, let alone walk.

At four a.m. we were on the move again

'Where are you taking us,' I asked a guard.

'We're taking you to Jebel Ali police station, Mr. Peter, get back on the bus.'

At that stage I was like child being told what to do having totally submitted to the guards' control and offering no resistance. Jebel Ali is where I almost lost my mind.

The incident that very nearly pushed me into the realms of

total madness was a Jebel Ali police officer telling me I couldn't be released because I still had an outstanding case against me: 'a big case, a very big case,' he put it, emphasising the word: 'big.'

The sadistic bastard enjoyed every moment as he watched my shocked reaction.

I couldn't understand what he was talking about. 'What big case?' I asked.

He had no clear answer and I had no choice but to hunker down in a cubicle and wait for something to happen.

After an hour or so, whether it was the total collapse of my emotional strength, or the searing, bright, fluorescent lights, I had a terrifying feeling I was losing it and about to go mad like my late friend, Peter, at court back in 2010.

'I can't take much more of this,' I sobbed to myself fearing I was about to break down and start punching someone.

Then guards hustled me upstairs to a chamber with five Indian, four Arab and a lone Pakistani prisoner, already in it.

They'd been arrested for drink driving earlier in the day and some were still pissed.

What a fucking bizarre scenario, I thought. There was I about to go mad and they'd pushed me in a room with ten drunks.

I found myself a bunk and slept for twelve hours straight.

I need to push my story on a bit here and say that the long sleep alongside the snoring drunks did me the world of good.

I'd also been able get hold of my brother-in-law, Karsten, by telephone and asked him to send me a small amount of money and essentials like toothpaste and soap.

Karsten is a top man and the emergency supplies I requested arrived in time just before, days later, I was shipped off to Central Police Headquarters where it emerged the so-called big case still outstanding against me wasn't a criminal matter at all. It was a civil case brought by the pilots to recover their missing U.S.$7 million from the failed construction deal.

There was another problem stopping me leaving Dubai.

It emerged in civil court that unbeknown to me I'd been served with a deportation order which couldn't be executed because I didn't have a passport! I guessed the lack of paperwork, was the real reason they weren't letting me go, not the pending civil case.

Like Christ in the wilderness, the back and forth shuttling between police stations went on for forty days and forty nights, give or take. Again, in the spirit of keeping this sorry tale interesting to an outsider, can I conclude by telling you more than five weeks after leaving Dubai Central, having said my goodbyes, thinking I was being set free, they bussed me back inside again.

Luckily, my old bunk in B Block was still free.

20

Half-way house

As I mentioned in early chapters, Dubai Central jail complex, in the Al-Awir desert is one of the biggest in the Middle East and in one section is a facility we inmates knew as the: Out-Jail.

I never knew its official title in Arabic.

The Out-Jail was not only a prison for minor offenders like shoplifters, but also a sort of half-way house for long term inmates like me who were set to be released but for some bureaucratic reason or another didn't have the right paperwork.

I'd been moved there in October 2017, keeping my hopes burning they were going to let me go at some point, although I was disappointed to hear one inmate, due for release, had been marooned there two-and-a-half years. However, let's not talk about him!

There's an incredible guy running the Out-Jail and to this day I believe he still does.

He's a Brit guy called Richard, who is in his forties, built like a brick shithouse, a former boxing champion and one of the best guys I've ever met.

Bizarrely, he's an inmate serving a long stretch for bounced checks.

You're probably wondering why a prisoner is a *de facto*

governor of a jail? I couldn't fully work it out either, but the authorities valued his administration skills, put him in charge and thought he was doing a grand job.

The Out-Jail was like chalk and cheese to the main Dubai Central prison blocks I'd been held in.

There are eight wings with ninety male prisoners in each, mostly Asians from the Philippines and Pakistan and a fair sprinkling of Arabs.

And while the main jail had no facilities in cells, other than bunk beds, the Out-Jail was luxurious by comparison.

I was astonished to find chairs, microwaves, even toasters! There was a decent weights room, too, and running machines! My jaw fell in surprise as I took my first grand tour.

Overall the atmosphere was much less oppressive than the main jail, with some of the younger inmates detailed to serve meals, teas and coffees.

Still not a holiday camp, by any standards, but I could hack it, especially as the running around by officialdom to sort out my release papers seemed to be building to a crescendo.

Some nonsense over a last-minute civil case had stopped me leaving earlier in the year: that was sorted.

And a rogue bail application, which I won't trouble you with, was also dispatched to the legal dustbin.

Eventually Out-Jail boss Richard came up to me at the end of November 2017 and said: 'Peter, you're going home!'

21

Glass of champagne, sir?

I clutched the Qantas ticket in my fist. I wasn't going to let it go, 2.40 a.m. departure Wednesday, November 29th 2017, Dubai Terminal Three to London Heathrow.

Back of the freaking net! Could this be true? Was this really happening?

I was so happy I couldn't stop singing.

After eight years and ten months behind bars, it seemed I was finally going home.

My loyal, wonderful, brother-in-law, Karsten, had bought the ticket and about 9 p.m. Tuesday evening I left Out-Jail in a prison van with two other inmates also being deported.

Or was I? I still had massive doubts. After all the promises, the false starts, the last-minute hitches, I felt sure my release might all go tits up at some point and they'd shunt me back to Dubai Central to finish what was a life sentence.

The next four or five hours were a blur.

It was dark and of course we weren't normal air passengers. The van disappeared into a maze of airport buildings to which the public don't normally have access.

I had to judge where we were by sense of sound and smell because I couldn't see out of the van. Occasionally, I'd catch a whiff of aviation fuel and hear the whine and almighty roar of a jetliner's engines as planes took off, so we obviously were, pretty close, to the runways on a meandering odyssey through various security checkpoints.

Eventually a jerk of brakes and we parked-up by an anonymous hut and the guards shouted: '*Yellah!* go,' 'You go now,' as they opened the van's metal cage.

The three of us stepped out of the van, our handcuffs were removed and one of the guards handed me my precious British passport.

'Go! You go now!' the guard repeated impatiently.

To my joy I suddenly saw Karsten standing there in the shadows. He had a broad smile.

'It's over, Peter, it's over,' he said with a catch in his voice as we hugged.

'I just wanted to be here to see you caught your flight.'

I was speechless and embraced him again.

'You'd better go now. Ring me when you get to London.'

The next few minutes were surreal as guards directed me down a gloomy corridor.

By that stage I felt I could have been walking toward the edge of a cliff like a lemming.

In one sense I did, because as I neared the end of the dark corridor unseen automatic doors slid open and found myself, on my own, metaphorically catapulted into the midst of freaking duty free! The neon blinded me for a moment.

Anyone who's familiar with Dubai airport knows what a three-ring-circus duty free is: thumping music, pretty girls selling perfume, piles of tawdry souvenir camels and models of the Burj Al Khalifa tower, busy outlets like Harrods and hordes of passengers snapping up alcohol, cigarettes and electrical goods like the world was about to end.

For a moment the noise and general confusion was too much for me. Remember, I'd been in jail nearly nine years.

But I was prevented, from doing an about-turn to the institutionalised world I'd left behind because the sliding doors had snapped shut behind me.

For some minutes I stood in duty free looking lost and alone, dressed in grubby slacks and a shirt and clutching a plastic bag with my prison toiletries like toothbrush, towel and soap.

Other passengers were too busy shopping and scurrying to waiting planes to notice me, although I had a sudden urge to scream: 'Look at me, folks! I'm Peter Margetts, I've just been released early from a life sentence, but during my time behind bars I witnessed the gruesome murder of a mob boss, nearly killed myself on hunger strike, mixed with some of the world's most notorious criminals, I watched a child killer being taken out to be shot, I lost my dad, but couldn't attend his funeral, other friends in jail died mysteriously, I've met a Nazi hunter and a football legend, Maradona, I'm bankrupt, and now my wife wants a divorce.

'But look at me, you sods! I'm fucking free at last!'

As I joined other passengers and walked down the ramp toward the London-bound Qantas Airbus 380 I still feared some bastard would suddenly leap out of a doorway to stop me leaving, or there'd be a previously unknown and unresolved paperwork problem that would prevent me boarding.

I mean, this wasn't really happening! Right?

I reached the plane's door and stepped aboard where a big, beautiful Aussie stewardess, in her twenties with bouncing blonde hair, greeted me and examined my boarding pass.

'Good evening, Mr. Margetts. Welcome on board. Ah, yes, aisle seat down there please.'

Then: 'Oh, no, Mr. Margetts, stop, wait a moment, sir. Wait there.'

'There's a problem,' she said, giving my boarding pass closer scrutiny.

I can tell you, at that point, I nearly shat my pants ten times over.

'I knew it.' I thought. 'I've been fucked over by those Dubai bastards. They're not letting me go. Blondie's going to call airport security, they're going to send me back to jail.'

A myriad of mad thoughts rushed through my mind. I also started shaking. Even my dodgy eye flickered.

'Mr. Margetts, I'm so sorry to tell you.'

'Yes,' I interrupted her.

'I'm sorry, but there's a mechanical problem with your seat! We've got engineers working on it now, trying to fix it. I do apologise,' she added, flashing a broad smile.

'Meanwhile, would you like to come upstairs to first class and have a glass of champagne on us?'

Did I ever!

I followed her, beautifully curved body, as we climbed upstairs to the bar in first class where she poured me a wonderful glass of bubbly, the first alcohol I tasted in almost nine years.

'How's the champagne Mr. Margetts?'

I remained silent for a moment, looked into her luscious brown eyes and mumbled,

'You will never know…you will never know.'

The moment of my release, prison guards deposit me at Dubai Airport to catch a flight home

Reunited with my precious daughter, Olivia.

22

Thanks, Lady A

Throughout this book I've told how I struggled like crazy against Dubai's legal system to win my freedom, how my case was raised at the highest government level in the UK and the UAE and how I used other ways to get released, like me applying to the Ruler's Court.

But what was it that finally persuaded them to let me go so suddenly?

I think I found the answer in London when I visited my MP Zac Goldsmith to thank him for all his help.

Zac, you'll remember, entered the picture when my pro-bono lawyers John Cookson and Richard Gray drew my case to his attention.

The appointment with Zac was at Portcullis House next to the House of Commons in mid-January 2018, a couple of months after my release where I waited in the foyer with his assistant.

Then, in he came. We'd never met before and he was more dashing and taller than I expected.

Zac was remarkably down to earth; he said how pleased he was I'd been freed; asked me about my health, a little about the ordeal of the last nine years, what my plans were, how my family had reacted, and so on.

Then my key question: 'Did he know why I'd suddenly been freed?'

'Well I'll tell you this, Peter,' said Zac.

'I know my mother Lady Annabel telephoned Sheikh Mohammed personally and basically said you'd been held long enough.'

'Three days later I got a missed call from the UAE and three days after that I heard from powers that be in Dubai you were being freed.

'That's all I can tell you.'

So, we'll never know for sure. And maybe it will always be a mystery.

But if it was down to your intervention Lady Annabel, as seems likely; from the bottom of my heart: a million thanks.

23

My darling Olivia

It was a crisp morning in early December when my flight from London landed in another European capital where I knew Susan and my precious daughter, Olivia, waited for me in the arrivals' hall.

I've agreed with Susan for the purposes of this book not to divulge exactly where she's started her new life.

I'd only been released from jail a few days and every hour of my new-found freedom was like drinking the elixir of life. After almost nine years locked up, the London I'd just left behind had seemed so fast, so modern; new fashions, modern taxis, buses, cyclists, bustling pavements; it was all difficult to take in. So much had changed.

I cleared passport control and soon spotted Susan in the arrivals' hall. The last time I'd seen her was in 2012 when I'd been on hunger strike and both she and Olivia had been allowed to visit me in jail. Olivia would not have a clear memory of that, she'd been too young.

You'll recall from earlier chapters Susan had hinted our marriage was finished, but she'd assured me she wouldn't stand in the way of my relationship with Olivia.

Our eyes met. My wife looked forlorn, and it was then I

realised the loving relationship I'd once had was over. But where was Olivia?

'She's over there,' said Susan with a half-smile and pointed to a newsagents.

Among the magazines and books, I saw her, my darling girl, now a young lady, ten years old.

I walked over just as she looked up at me; her face, pale and beautiful

'I'm home honey, it's Daddy!'

There was no hesitation. We cuddled each other, waves of emotion washed over us both.

As I hugged Olivia, I'd never felt closer to any human than I did at that moment. Olivia said nothing. Poor kid, it must have been so overwhelming. Here was a man she hardly knew, suddenly in her life and holding her tight.

And Olivia stayed pretty quiet, as Susan and I drove in my wife's car to their home, where I hoped I'd begin renewing my relationship and start making up for the lost years.

All credit to Susan, bringing a child up on her own with little money, in Europe, must have been very tough. And it's a huge tribute to her that Olivia had grown to be such a polite, loving and caring young lady.

Susan had protected Olivia from the truth about her daddy being in jail by telling her I was away on a special mission. That story had worked with Olivia, and the neighbors, until Olivia was about six. Then she had started saying to Susan: 'When's Daddy coming home? Even soldiers who go away come back again.'

Susan used to reply: 'Yes, my love. He is coming home, and when he does, he won't leave you again.'

The days that followed were pure bliss. I picked Olivia up from school every day, although I was a bit unnerved, by something she said one afternoon.

I had a business meeting in the UK for a day or two. Olivia gripped my hand and said,

'You will come back, won't you Daddy?'

I embraced her and said, 'Of course I will my love.'

I returned from the UK in time to go with Susan and Olivia to my daughter's Christmas Carol concert. It was very emotional, and I cried.

That Christmas was truly special. I drove Olivia to a youth club near her home. All her friends, about six of seven of them around her own age, were milling around outside.

Olivia and I got out of the car and Olivia said,

'Look everybody, this is my Daddy.'

Then we all cuddled.

For every journey there is an end, and after nine years, mine was finally over.

POSTSCRIPT

In November 2017, a landmark legal decision in Dubai downgraded the offense of writing a non-fraudulent bounced check to the status of misdemeanor or simple crime to be dealt with in a fast-track one day tribunal, not the criminal courts.

In the case of a non-fraudulent bounced check with a value of U.S.$55,000, or less, offenders would no longer be sent to jail, but fined up to U.S.$2,700.

This key ruling put an end to business folk like Peter Margetts going to prison, and also spelled the end of Dubai's hated security check system.

FINAL THOUGHTS

by Peter Margetts

First and foremost this book is dedicated to my beautiful daughter, Olivia. I hope you will understand why I was away and how much I missed you.

To my wife Susan: thanks for your support when I was released. I'm not sure how that journey would have panned out without your help and love.

To brother-in-law, Karsten, Linda and family: Karsten, you are the best person I have ever met. You helped me through the bad times and stuck by me when everyone had left. I love you all.

To our two dogs, Buddy and Rudy. Rudy you sat outside for a week waiting for me in Dubai. You were there for me when I came home.

To my natural mother, Bridget McGivney: I understand.

I am eternally grateful to:
Denise Mitchell in California.
Tracey and all your family: thanks for your warmth and your acceptance of me.
Ann and Kevin: thanks for the support particularly when I was on hunger strike.

Magda and Mike: you have always been there for me. Kisses.

Jezzie B: Thanks for propping me up after release when I was floundering like Bambi on ice.

Ian aka Slip and family: health and happiness buddy.

Gemma R and family glad you have found happiness x.

Thanks to friends who appeared along the way and then disappeared:

Karen C and Richard G.

Prison friends I can never forget:

Arshad Tikara: the help you gave me over the years, the infectious smile that came throughout your nineteen-year journey, I'm sure there are many hundreds of prisoners, like me, who want to thank you.

Malik Bashir: my Libyan friend. I hope to see you in London, one day.

Wail Hamed: what happened to you is a book in itself, like the next four mentioned.

Ryan Cornelius and Charles Ridley: Thanks for teaching us rugby and apologies about the football mentality! One day you will be free and it's the next book on the list. I haven't forgotten.

Richard Hamilton: I hope by the time this is published you're out to see your lovely family.

Mark: Mate, the friendship I shared with you I'll never forget. Mark, I understand everything. Get in touch and I'm there. Best footballer by far, even better than the ex-pros like Faysal and the French crew. Some great games released us from the monotony of life in Central Jail.

To all the guys who played football with me over the years in jail. We had some great games and a few fights, but at day's end we were all brothers on the concrete square.

Respect to: Prince, Faysal, Kamal, Ibrahim *The Terminator*, Neil W R, Millwall Steve, Spud and all the local Emirati prisoners who tried to break my legs at first, then calmed down!

Thanks to people on the outside who always answered: John Catterill and family Andrew Docherty and family, Nick Tromans and family, Paul S and family. Without you all I would not have made it. Thank you for getting me through the journey.

Since my release I've bumped into old friends and had some emotional chats. 'This is Peter who I told you about,' my friend said to his son. There have been many of those meetings. One said: 'I read about you!'

I came across a university friend in a supermarket a few months ago. He went white as a ghost when he saw me. 'I thought you were never coming out!' he said.

I'd like to thank all my uni friends: Emma, Steve, Richie and Chris P.

And to all my Leeds United family: every one of you, our bond will never be broken. Are Leeds marching on together?! Come on! (There are so many of our crew that I'm not going to name anyone for fear of insulting the people I'd have missed out.)

Prison is never easy, only made bearable by the people you meet on the inside and who become your extended family. When you are on the inside, the outside world is only entered when you call and connect with someone.

There are so many of you I can't mention you all by name, but you know who you are. To all my fellow prisoners I've met over the years: I hope everything works out in your lives and I thank you for sharing time with me.

To Hassan Mohammed Sadri: You started the domino effect, the financial crisis just re-fuelled it.

Finally, my deep thoughts to the guys who've fallen while in the custody of Dubai's penal system: Jonny Jouty, Peter Kane, Lee Bradley Brown. RIP.